BRAVEST
OF THE BRAVE
THE STORY OF THE
VICTORIA
CROSS

JOHN GLANFIELD

SUTTON PUBLISHING

First published in the United Kingdom in 2005 by
Sutton Publishing Limited · Phoenix Mill
Thrupp · Stroud · Gloucestershire · GL5 2BU

Reprinted 2006

British Library Cataloguing in Publication Data
A catalogue record for this book is available from the British Library.

ISBN 0-7509-3695-9

Typeset in 10.5/13.5pt Sabon.
Typesetting and origination by
Sutton Publishing Limited.
Printed and bound in England by
J.H. Haynes & Co. Ltd, Sparkford.

*To the Bravest of the Brave,
in awe and gratitude*

They fled only from dishonour,
but met danger face to face.

Pericles

Contents

List of Illustrations

IWM Imperial War Museum
VCS The Victoria Cross Society

Acknowledgements

Thanks first to Jonathan Falconer, who commissioned me to write this book. His enthusiasm and unfailing support are much appreciated.

Of the many who helped so willingly with research, guidance and timely encouragement, my grateful thanks to Brian Best of the Victoria Cross Society and editor of its journal for his invaluable contribution, pictorial and historical. Sincere thanks also to William Spencer, ever-helpful military specialist at The National Archives, Kew; David Callaghan, past director of Hancocks, makers of the Victoria Cross; John Hayward, Executive Consultant to Spink & Son Ltd; Brig Ken Timbers, Chairman of the Royal Artillery Historical Trust; Mark Smith, Curator of the Royal Artillery Museum, Woolwich, and Matthew Buck its Researcher; David Starley and Philip Abbott for their labours and welcome revelations at Leeds Armouries; likewise Dr Kevin Clancy, Librarian and Curator at The Royal Mint; Dr Geoffrey Parnell, Keeper of Tower History, and Henry Firmin, Tower of London; David Fletcher, Archivist and matchless oracle at Bovington Tank Museum; Barbara Tomlinson, Curator of Antiquities, and Bob Todd, Head of Historic Photographs, National Maritime Museum; Darran Cowd and Peter Elliott, RAF Museum Hendon; Mrs Sue Lines, David Owen and Erika Spencer at the Royal Logistic Corps Museum; Andrew Currey at the Australian War Memorial, Canberra; Anthony Staunton, editor of *Sabretache*, the journal of the Military Historical Society of Australia; Fiona Nelson, Phil Brouwer and Sandra Hough of the Institute of Materials Engineers, Australia; Lesley Smurthwaite and Teresa Watts,

National Army Museum; Gavin Edgeley-Harris, Curator, the Gurkha Museum, and Lt Col John Darroch at The Royal Hampshire Regiment Museum, both in Winchester; Chaz Bowyer, air historian; Yvonne Oliver and Alan Wakefield at the Imperial War Museum; the Revd Canon David Marshall, Lambeth Palace; the Trustees of the Regimental and Chattels Charity of the former Durham Light Infantry, and Jennifer Gill, County Archivist, the Durham County Record Office.

I am particularly grateful to Colin Sibun, Director of the Army Museums Ogilby Trust, which holds the copyright to Michael J. Crook's *The Evolution of the Victorian Cross*, for permission to draw on this scholarly work. Hilary Walford, Nick Reynolds and Martin Latham of Sutton Publishing have ensured the book's smooth passage through their always friendly and professional attentions, for which my very warmest thanks. Though many have contributed, responsibility for any error or misinterpretation is mine alone. Last but above all, my thanks to my dear wife, Caroline, for her encouragement and forbearance, willingly given for many moons.

Introduction
'A little bit of ribbon'

The value attached by soldiers to a little bit of ribbon
is such as to render any danger insignificant and any
privation light, if it can be attained, and I believe that
great indeed would be the stimulus and deeply prized
the reward of a Cross of Military Merit.

(Secretary of State for War Lord Newcastle
to Prince Albert, 20 January 1855)

There was no such thing as a gallantry award for British
servicemen and their junior officers at the start of the
Crimean War in 1854. They were required to do their duty – to
stand fast and fight bravely. To decorate men for doing no more
than their duty would signal that duty had become optional.

This military mindset was about to be challenged by rising
public anger. The novel presence of newspaper correspondents
with the Army brought graphic battle reports from the Crimea.
There was a growing realisation at home that war is not
glorious but frightful, and that those who were fighting and
dying for Queen and country were not 'the sweepings of the
gutter' but fiercely brave and loyal men. Popular demand grew
for a gallantry medal open to all ranks. The Victoria Cross was
accordingly instituted in 1856 and awarded retrospectively to
heroes of the Crimean War. It became and remains Britain's
supreme decoration for those who 'in the presence of the Enemy
shall have performed some signal act of valour or devotion
to their Country'. Courage alone is not enough to gain the

much-coveted Cross. It is worn before all other orders, decorations and medals and has earned worldwide respect.

The great gallantry of the 1,351 men who have won the VC, three of whom gained Bars, was well defined by Dr Rowan Williams, Archbishop of Canterbury, at the dedication of the memorial to holders of the Victoria Cross and the George Cross in Westminster Abbey on 14 May 2003: 'there is more to bravery than heroic insanity. The courage of mind and heart comes not just from patriotism but from conviction that a country is committed to justice or freedom. Not just from obedience to orders or to some abstract duty, but from a sense of the human worthwhileness of comrades and colleagues.'

The author's wish to know more about those to whom we owe so much, and about the underlying story of the Victoria Cross itself, came about when he was privileged to lunch with HM the Queen Mother and holders of the Cross at London's Royal Tournament. The quietly spoken recollections of Lt-Cdr Ian Fraser VC, DSC, RD and Bar, whose midget submarine had crippled a Japanese heavy cruiser at its moorings, were those of a man who believed he was simply doing a job. It typified their invariable modesty and was an inspiring and humbling experience for the listener.

Here then is an account of the acts of supreme gallantry and endurance of some of those exceptional men. It is inseparable from the sometimes idiosyncratic story of the Victoria Cross itself, the coveted 'little bit of ribbon' by which for a century and a half the nation and Commonwealth have honoured the Bravest of their Brave.

1

The Crimean War, 1854–1856

> I suppose we shall have leather medals for this one
> day – I mean those who have the good fortune to
> escape the shot and shell of the enemy and the
> pestilence that surrounds us.
>
> *(Sgt Timothy Gowing, Royal Fusiliers.*
> *Letter home from the Crimea, 29 October 1854)*

A singularly ill-equipped and ill-fated British Army sailed for the Crimea and war with Russia in 1854. The fighting spirit and discipline of its 27,000 mostly inexperienced troops and their junior officers proved formidable. Lord Raglan the C in C had seen no action for forty years since losing his right arm at Waterloo. Many of his hand-picked generals would fail him and their troops. The bureaucratic tangle of supply departments on which all relied were grotesquely inefficient. When the survivors came home two years later they left behind 4,800 killed in action or died of wounds, and another 17,000 dead from disease and, too often, sheer neglect.

Britain and France had declared war on Russia in support of Turkey and its crumbling empire, threatened by the Tsar's ambitions. The British feared that the Russian fleet bottled up in the Black Sea would break out into the Mediterranean through the Turkish-held Dardanelles Straits to menace British trade routes to India and the Far East. France had its own territorial ambitions. The Allies determined to sink Russia's Black Sea fleet and destroy its naval base at Sebastopol on the Crimean peninsula. Lord Raglan's force joined Marshal Saint-Arnaud's French army of 30,000, attached to which were 7,000 Turkish infantry. The Allies' 63,000 men faced comparable strength in Gen Prince Alexander Mentschikoff's Russian field army.

This was the first European war to be attended by correspondents for British newspapers, most notably William Howard Russell of *The Times*. The 35-year-old Irishman's vivid dispatches gripped the nation, fuelling an overwhelming demand for a gallantry medal open to all ranks. The Victoria Cross, Britain's supreme decoration for valour, was instituted by Royal Warrant in January 1856. The first 111 VCs were awarded regardless of rank for acts of conspicuous gallantry in the cauldron of the Crimea, and on the high seas. The following speak for all.

The Baltic, 21 June 1854

Midshipman (A/Mate) Charles Lucas RN

A 20-year-old sailor from Armagh holds the distinction of performing the first act to earn the Victoria Cross in what was almost the first engagement of the war. An Anglo-French fleet had been sent to the Baltic to destroy Russia's main fleet and mount a blockade. When the Russian navy refused to leave its Kronstadt base and give fight, the Allied squadrons resorted to spoiling attacks on shore defences. During one of these the quick thinking of Charles Lucas, Midshipman and Acting Mate of the 8-gun paddle sloop *Hecla*, saved many lives. The *Hecla* was bombarding the shore batteries of a large Russian fortress at Bomarsund in the Aland islands on 21 June 1854. Lucas had charge of the guns, the two largest of which were lobbing 84lb shells at enemy emplacements only 500yd distant.

As the Russians returned fire a heavy shell crashed onto *Hecla*'s open gun deck, its fuse burning. Explosive shells were essentially hollowed cannon balls, powder-filled and primitively fused. Ignoring shouted warnings, Lucas ran at the smoking missile, whose fuse had been cut to length by its gunners according to range to ensure it exploded close on impact. He was gambling on a miscalculation, theirs or his. Gathering it up he ran to the rail and heaved it over. The shell exploded thunderously on the waterline, slightly injuring two crewmen. Lucas, a gunner himself, well knew the odds he faced at the moment of decision. Capt William Hall immediately promoted him to lieutenant and recommended him for an award in recognition of his gallantry and selfless disregard. Years later Lucas married Hall's daughter. He ended his naval career as a rear-admiral. After a train journey probably in 1878/9 he was shocked to find he had left all his medals in the carriage. They were never recovered. An un-inscribed duplicate group was issued, including the VC. When Lucas died in August 1914, it was donated to the National Maritime Museum.

Battle of the Alma, 20 September 1854

Sgt Luke O'Connor. Capt Edward Bell

The Allies landed unopposed on 14 September, 30 miles north of Sebastopol. They reached the Alma river on the 20th. Across it Raglan's men saw walled vineyards rising to open ground and a 300ft-high ridge crowned by their main objective, a heavy battery of 32pdr howitzers in the Great Redoubt. The French and Turks on their right had first to capture the heights to seaward. Mentschikoff had eighty guns and close to 20,000 troops fronting the British. So confident was he that residents from Sebastopol were permitted to climb the ridge to watch, leaving a scatter of bonnets and parasols when later they ran for their lives.

The British lay waiting under increasingly punishing fire until Raglan lost patience, ordering his regiments forward in a raw frontal assault, no feints or flanking move. He crossed the river fearlessly with his officers, cheering the men on as grapeshot and canister broke many formations into disorganised groups. Officers attempted to rally them on their colours and re-form for the climb ahead. Eighteen-year-old Lt Anstruther of the 23rd Regiment (later the Royal Welsh Fusiliers) bravely carried its Colour until he was killed barely 40yd from the Redoubt. The silken flag passed to Sgt Luke O'Connor, who had just regained his feet after receiving a deflected shot in the chest. The advance had stalled under remorseless fire from cannon and small arms. The effectiveness of roundshot against men in depth could be devastating. One Russian ball killed fifteen in this assault. Ignoring the fusillade and the pain of his wound, O'Connor ran ahead and planted the Colour's pole in the Redoubt, to the astonishment of its defenders. His action spurred the battalion forward in support. They took the position at bayonet point with elements of the Guards and the Highlanders.

Observing the carnage, Russell of *The Times* reported that nevertheless 'individual escapes of officers and men are miraculous – chin straps were shot off, buttons carried away, belts torn, coats ripped up – all without further injury'. Encumbered with the heavy flag and already badly wounded, O'Connor had been immensely lucky to reach the earthwork. Lt Granville ordered him to the rear for treatment. The Irishman pleaded so earnestly to see it through that he got his way, carrying the Regiment's most potent symbol for the rest of that day. Lord Wolseley once remarked that 'the General who would condemn anyone to carry a large silk colour under close musketry fire ought to be tried for murder'. It was the plain truth. That evening twenty-six holes were counted in O'Connor's silk. His was the first action by a soldier to be rewarded with the VC. The citation coupled it with a second on 8 September 1855 when, as a newly commissioned lieutenant in the 23rd, and though shot through both thighs, he showed great gallantry during the attack on the Redan at Sebastopol. After long and distinguished service Luke O'Connor became honorary colonel of his old regiment. He died in 1915 aged 84.

Shortly before the Redoubt fell, its gunners limbered up in a frantic effort to save Russian ordnance and honour while riflemen at the embrasures gave covering fire. When Raglan's men overran the sprawling and smoke-logged earthwork,

Capt Edward Bell of the 23rd glimpsed at the far end a gun team attempting to remove the last 32pdr, its driver furiously whipping up the only three horses they had got into traces. Bell ran at him, ordering him at pistol point to turn the team round and head for the river. The Russian fled. Bell and Fusilier Cpl Pye seized the horses and triumphantly led their prize away. They were spotted by Lt-Gen Sir George Brown, commander of the Light Division and a martinet, arguably the most disliked officer in the British Army. Enraged, and ignoring the gun, he ordered the Captain back to his company in language enriched with a veteran's vocabulary. Bell further distinguished himself that day, at last leading the Regiment out of action when all its senior officers had fallen.

The fine gun on a pale green carriage was the first effective field piece to be captured by the British. It was known as 'Bell's gun', and went in 1885 to the brigade depot at Wrexham to stand before the officers' mess. For his quick-thinking gallantry that day Bell was awarded the Victoria Cross. After service at Lucknow during the Indian Mutiny he attained the rank of major-general and command of the Belfast Division.

Eight VCs were gained above the Alma. Over the next two days the British recovered some 2,000 wounded and buried 362 dead. French casualties were 63 killed and 500 wounded. Russian losses exceeded 5,000 including 1,810 dead. A Russian officer remarked during a later truce: 'You won a brilliant victory at the Alma.'

Balaclava, 25 October 1854

Sgt-Maj John Grieve. Sgt Henry Ramage. Sgt-Maj John Berryman. Sgt John Farrell. Lance-Sgt Joseph Malone. Cpl Charles Wooden. Surgeon James Mouat. Pte Samuel Parkes. Lt Alexander Dunn

Finding Sebastopol's northern defences impregnable, the Allies undertook a bold flanking march to Balaclava 3 miles beyond the city. The small town and its harbour were quickly taken, and the French seized another. When bombardment to reduce Sebastopol's defence works proved ineffective, the Allies dug in for an unexpected siege war. The Russians fought to regain Balaclava before the first snows, knowing that loss of the harbour supplying Raglan's men would starve the British into submission in the depths of a Crimean winter.

Balaclava is remembered for the extraordinary gallantry and tragic waste surrounding a single event, the charge of the Light Cavalry Brigade on 25 October. The 'Death Ride of the 600' earned seven Victoria Crosses. Two more were secured earlier that morning in a brilliantly successful but almost forgotten charge by Dragoons of the Heavy Brigade. Gen Liprandi had attacked out of the east at dawn with 25,000 men, striking the British right flank and capturing Turkish-manned batteries on a ridge separating the long North and South valleys. Russian cavalry then wheeled off the ridge into South Valley to strike Maj-Gen Sir Colin Campbell's final defence line before Balaclava, while the 1,500 sabres of Maj-Gen Lord Lucan's Cavalry Division awaited orders at the valley's distant western end. Raglan commanded Lucan to detach eight squadrons of Dragoons to assist the defenders. Brig-Gen Sir James Scarlett, the Heavy Cavalry Brigade's 55-year-old commander, braced himself for his first-ever combat.

Campbell's Highlanders beat off the attack before Scarlett's 600 Dragoons could reach them. However, Russian lances were soon pricking the skyline along the ridge to Scarlett's left as a mass of 1,600 cavalry breasted it and prepared to sweep down on his troopers. Scarlett shouted 'left wheel into line and form to charge uphill'. Turning their backs on the enemy, his troop officers prepared an extended line as if on exercise. The Russians halted in momentary disbelief, their first and second lines easily twice the length and three times the depth of the Heavy Brigade's. Calling to sound the charge, Scarlett led off with only the 6th Inniskillings and two squadrons of the Royal Scots Greys, barely 300 in all. The others followed some way behind after delay in crossing a vineyard. Scarlett was first in; then came the shock as the first squadrons crashed deep among them. They were too tightly bunched for lances; it was sword and pistol work for all. The Russians' thick overcoats gave protection against sweeping cuts and, reported Lt-Col Griffiths, 'when our men made a thrust with the sword they all bent and would not go into a man's body'. The straight English cavalry sword contrasted with the Russian's heavy curved blade, usually blunt as a poker. Amazingly, the Russians were beaten back to the ridge and driven off. Scarlett got away with a badly gashed hand and his clothing much cut about.

Sgt-Maj John Grieve, 2nd Dragoons (Royal Scots Greys), received his VC for riding to the rescue of an officer 'surrounded by the enemy who were slashing at him in the duly approved cowardly fashion of Muscovite troops', as one observer reported. Grieve cut off the head of the first at a blow, before disabling and dispersing the rest. He expected no reward, believing it was all in a day's work. He was later commissioned and became adjutant of his old regiment.

Grieve's comrade-in-arms Sgt Henry Ramage gained the VC for a series of acts of gallantry that day. He first saved the life of Pte M'Pherson, also of the 2nd Dragoons, by galloping to disperse seven Cossacks who surrounded him. As the enemy withdrew and the Brigade rallied, Ramage's fine grey horse refused to leave the ranks. Ramage dismounted and took the opportunity to chase and capture a prisoner. Later, under intense fire, he rescued a badly wounded Light Brigade trooper. Ramage survived the war, only to die within five years aged 32.

Later that morning Raglan's loosely worded and carelessly conveyed order misdirected Lucan into a catastrophic blunder. Instead of sending the Earl of Cardigan's Light Brigade up to the ridge on its right as Raglan desired, to stop the Russians hauling away their newly captured guns, Lucan dispatched some 640 men on the epic but pointless charge down the North Valley. At the far end Liprandi's cavalry was regrouping behind a screen of waiting guns. The Brigade's Light Dragoons, Hussars and Lancers raced over a mile through a blast of fire from the battery ahead of them and from guns and rifles on the heights to either side. Cardigan's much-thinned first line broke in front of the battery, the second line merging with it as they cut down the gunners who had not fled, before racing on to engage the Russian cavalry. The remnants of the Brigade were eventually beaten back, pursued by Lancers. The wounded and the otherwise unhorsed stood no chance. French colonial cavalry raced to protect Cardigan's left flank, silencing fourteen guns on the escarpment after a brilliant but costly charge.

Sgt-Maj John Berryman, 17th Lancers, had his bay mare shot under him at the battery. Wounded in the calf, he managed to catch and mount a loose charger, which was brought down moments later. He crouched as two squadrons of the 11th Hussars charged past on either side, then started to the rear through fallen men and horses. He spotted Capt 'Peck' Webb of the 17th in great pain from a leg wound and unable to ride further. Lt George Smith, also unhorsed, helped him ease Webb to the ground, before making off on the Captain's charger to fetch a stretcher. Berryman remained with Webb under heavy fire, the guns having opened again, ignoring Webb's urging to leave him while there was time. Berryman hailed Sgt John Farrell of the 17th, also on foot, and with Lance-Sgt Joseph Malone of the 13th Light Dragoons they carried Webb in a stumbling half-run 200yds through the fall of shell, until they found a bearer party. A tourniquet was applied to Webb's thigh, then a stretcher was grabbed from two band boys and the little group moved on under fire. The French Cavalry Commander Gen Maurice met them, exclaiming: 'Ah! And you Sergeant. If you were in the French service I would make you an officer on the spot.' It was all for nothing, Capt Webb died days later. Berryman removed his boot to find it full of blood and a piece 'the size of a shilling' cut clean out of his calf, which became septic, taking many weeks to heal.

Berryman, Farrel and Malone survived the war to receive the Victoria Cross.

The 17th Lancers had paraded 140 strong before the charge. Afterwards they mustered 34. Capt William Morris had led them until his capture, escape, and the loss of two horses killed, left him badly wounded in an exposed position close to the British end of the valley. For how long is unclear, but an attempt by Turkish troops to carry him in was abandoned when the Russians opened fire. When the news reached the Light Brigade, Cpl Charles Wooden of the 17th volunteered to accompany Surgeon James Mouat, 6th Dragoons, to bring him back. The two carried Morris to safety through a considerable fire. He recovered, only to die four years later in India. Mouat received the VC. Wooden, a big red-bearded quick-tempered German and a good soldier, was nicknamed 'Tish me – the Devil', his thick exclamation on being challenged by a sentry and forgetting the password after a drinking session. He had expected nothing, but on hearing of Mouat's award he wrote to remind him of his part in recovering Webb. Mouat forwarded the letter with his own recommendation to Horse Guards. It was reluctantly approved on grounds of fairness, and Wooden duly received the Cross. James Mouat became Surgeon to the Queen. Wooden was commissioned and joined the 6th (Inniskilling) Dragoons. Years later he was found bleeding in his Dover quarters, having shot himself in the head. He told the doctor who attended that he had tried to shoot out a badly aching tooth and the bullet had deflected. A small pocket pistol beside him had been fired twice. It looked more like attempted suicide but this was not pursued. Charles Wooden died next day, 26 April 1876.

When his horse collapsed from exhaustion, Trumpet Maj Crawford of the 4th Light Dragoons fell with it, losing his sword. He lay trapped as two Cossacks rode at him. They were seen by 6ft-2in Pte Samuel Parkes, 41, also of the 4th and likewise unhorsed. He ran at them and laid about him to such effect that they galloped off. As the two Dragoons followed the Brigade in retreat under indiscriminate fire, Crawford and Parkes were attacked by six more Russians. With one sword standing between them and butchery, Parkes fought off the attackers until they fled and his sword was shot out of his hand. The two were joined by trooper John Eddon, and later found Maj Halkett, too badly wounded to stand. Parkes heaved him across his shoulder and pressed on until exhaustion overtook him. A Russian officer called on them to surrender. When Parkes refused, he was shot in the hand before he and Crawford were captured. Later, noticing the tall well-set-up Parkes, Gen Liprandi commented sardonically: 'If you're a Light Dragoon what sort of men are your Heavy Dragoons?' Sam Parkes rejoined his regiment a year later and was the first Charger to receive the Cross from the Queen.

The Light Brigade's seventh and last VC that day was gained by 21-year-old Lt Alexander Roberts Dunn, 11th Hussars, the first Canadian to win the Cross. As tall as Parkes and with a mighty reach, Dunn had laid about him with a non-regulation 4ft sabre forged specially by Wilkinson. The regiment, splendid in their gold-braided blue jackets and crimson trousers, continued far beyond the battery to engage Russian cavalry in fierce fighting. When they were driven back under heavy musket fire from the right, Sgt Robert Bentley's injured charger fell behind. Dunn wordlessly turned his horse, a notorious kicker, and galloped back to see Bentley fighting off three Russian Dragoons. The two Hussars were the last of the Brigade there save the dead and dying. The rest of the 11th kept going, unaware of the plight of their comrades. Dunn sabred the first man off his horse, then turned to tackle the others, circling his wildly kicking mount as he hacked away. Having killed both he gallantly put the injured Bentley on his own horse before walking on alone. Dunn killed a Russian hussar attacking Pte Harvey Levett, also of the 11th, as he made his way back over the sprawled wreckage of the Brigade. He was judged a fine soldier by his peers, but a poor officer and a womaniser. Days later he applied to sell his commission before returning to family estates in Canada, taking his colonel's wife with him. In Dunn's absence he was voted for the Cross by his regiment and came to London to receive it, his colonel generously lending him his uniform for the occasion. In Canada Dunn helped raise and later commanded the 100th (Prince of Wales Royal Canadian) Regiment, bringing it to England in 1858. Colonel Dunn was serving in Abyssinia twenty years later when he accidentally shot himself dead while hunting.

The numbers of men who charged and who got back alive are disputed, but of the 640 or so who rode out, fewer than 375 returned after the 25-minute action. Nearly 500 horses were lost. The Brigade, literally the cutting edge of Raglan's expedition, never recovered as a fighting force in the Crimea. Gen Liprandi spoke for the astonished and admiring Russians, telling a group of prisoners 'You are noble fellows'.

The Naval Gunners, October 1854

A/Mate William Hewett RN

A/Mate William Hewett of the Royal Naval Brigade disobeyed orders in battle. Instead of a drumhead court martial and execution, he found himself a hero.

The Balaclava engagements had been followed next day, 26 October, by a Russian probing sortie. Liprandi dispatched 5,000 troops to test the British right flank of the Sebastopol siege line. A naval detachment with heavy ship's guns was present in support of Raglan's artillery. 'Nobby' Hewett, aged 20, commanded a 68pdr in a hilltop battery overlooking Sebastopol harbour. In bright afternoon sunshine the Russian force attacked posts to his right. Others followed ravines to reach the exposed rear of the battery, pouring in a sharp fire from Minié rifles at 300yd. The arc of fire of the big 'rifled' Lancasters was limited by their narrow embrasures, and the guns could not immediately be brought to bear. They were at imminent risk of being overwhelmed, when word was given to spike the guns and retire.

Hewett refused, saying that the order never came from Capt Lushington and he would not withdraw until it did. He ordered 'four handspikes, muzzle to the right', and with help from soldiers the gun weighing over 5 tons was swung until it lay hard against the low parapet wall of the battery. A messenger repeated the order to withdraw. 'Retire? Be damned – Fire!' Backed by a 16lb charge, the first shell blasted through the intervening parapet, punching a shrapnel spray of splinters from its stone-filled wicker baskets. Fire was steadily maintained by Hewett's crew until British infantry became mixed with the Russians, who were driven back in general retreat.

Mate Hewett was promoted to Lieutenant and given command of *Beagle*. He was again commended for exceptional bravery and leadership at the Battle of Inkerman on 5 November, bringing a double citation for award of the VC. Knighted in 1874, he ended his service as a notoriously irascible but respected rear admiral. He died in 1888 at Southsea, honoured at a huge funeral attended by ex-gunner Chiddle, the last surviving member of his Lancaster crew that day.

Sebastopol, June–September 1855

Lt Gerald Graham. Boatswain's Mate John Shepherd. Pte Alfred Ablett

Raglan's calamitous winter losses from sickness and sheer neglect were followed in the new year by much hard fighting, before 600 Allied siege guns in concert with those of the fleet opened a bombardment of Sebastopol's defences at dawn on Sunday 17 June. When they fell silent that evening 4,000 of Mentschikoff's defenders lay dead. Fresh troops were rushed up, emplacements frantically repaired and guns made ready for the inevitable Allied assault. It began prematurely next day with a mistimed pre-dawn attack by the French on the Malakoff fort. The Russians responded with an inferno of fire. By first light Saint-Arnaud's force had suffered a terrible slaughter. Raglan's planned assault of the Redan was timed for later that morning after his artillery had silenced its guns. Either he could order an immediate advance, or watch the French army bleed to death. Raglan dispatched his two waiting flank columns, each led by 100 riflemen with supporting engineers followed by ladder and storming parties. As they left their trenches to cross the intervening 400yd of open and mined ground, the Redan's untouched guns launched a firestorm so intense that men moved with heads bowed as in a gale. They were cut down in their hundreds. Few reached the walls. The disaster produced twelve VCs, most for braving the fire to bring in wounded. Other heroic actions would have gone unrecorded because all involved, including witnesses, were simply wiped out.

Engineer Lt Gerald Graham accompanied the ladder party of sailors in Gen Sir John Campbell's left-hand column of 500 men, plus 800 in reserve. Sir John was killed almost immediately, soon followed by Col Shadworth, his second in command. When Graham's party lost both its naval officers, the tall burly engineer led the men on until they were checked by the ferocity of the guns. As likely to die going back as forward, they pressed on at Graham's urging. With six sailors to each heavy ladder, and suffering casualties, they struggled to the abattis fronting the walls of the Redan to await the 400-strong storming party, which, unknown to them, had been cut to pieces. Graham miraculously got many of his men back to the trenches. His coolness and example inspired the sailors, who were notoriously wary of military officers. He left cover to bring in wounded under fire on numerous occasions during the siege. Graham's later distinguished service in India, China and Egypt brought him the thanks of both Houses of Parliament on three occasions. He retired as a lieutenant-general in 1890. We shall meet him again.

Four weeks after Graham's exploit, Boatswain's Mate John Shepherd literally launched a one-man war against Russian warships lying in Sebastopol's harbour just out of range of Allied guns. He proposed to sink Admiral Kornilov's flagship *Twelve Apostles* on his own – from a canoe. Shepherd had built the little craft with 3in of freeboard and camouflaged it with a painted canvas cover. He prepared to paddle across the busy and heavily guarded anchorage to fix a powerful explosive charge, knowing his chances of getting away were minimal. In trials his squadron was alerted to keep a sharp lookout. Next morning a dummy charge was found screwed to the forefoot of the British Admiral's flagship. Raglan and the Navy concluded that Shepherd's tactics were unsporting.

It was left to the French to borrow Shepherd and send him on his way from Careening Bay on the night of 15 July 1855 with 112lb of explosive. He paddled silently past sunken blockships and on into the harbour, where the little craft was halted by an endless chain of boats ferrying troops to the north side. Instead of turning back while it was dark, he lay there throughout the next day at imminent risk of discovery and death, noting enemy shipping and fortifications before making off at nightfall. Shepherd tried once more on 16 August, again thwarted by activity in the harbour. It was a hugely daring scheme. Had he succeeded, John Shepherd's name would be legendary. His VC was accompanied by the Légion d'Honneur. He was promoted to boatswain first class, and died aged 67 at Padstow in 1884.

A near-terminal accident accompanied Pte Alfred Ablett's disposal of a shell on 2 September. It lodged with burning fuse in the side of his trench next to barrels of powder and cases of ammunition. As the Grenadier Guardsman pulled the heavy iron ball away, it rolled between his legs, knocking him down. Ablett coolly recovered it and hurled it over the parapet, where it exploded on striking the ground. He was promoted to corporal, then sergeant, and received the VC from the Queen's hands. He was also presented with a silk necktie worked by Her Majesty. It was a touching and signal honour entirely in Victoria's gift, and rarely bestowed.

* * *

Sebastopol fell at last on 8 September after six great bombardments. Raglan never lived to see it. He died discredited and worn out, but bravely and with dignity. A peace treaty was signed in March 1856. Russia regained the Crimea, but its great naval base was destroyed and its fleet neutralised. Russia had lost half a million men, France and Turkey a hundred thousand each, and Britain 22,000 soldiers and sailors.

2

Valour's Cross

Here's Valour's Cross, my man, t'will serve,
Though rather ugly – take it.
John Bull a medal can deserve,
But can't contrive to make it.

(Anon. 1857)

Lacking an official gallantry award before the Victoria Cross was instituted in 1856, some senior officers introduced regimental decorations of their own. During the Peninsular War (1807–14) Col Belson of the 28th awarded certain of his men a crown worn on the sleeve above the chevrons with the letters 'VS' denoting 'Valiant Stormer'. Companionship of the Order of the Bath was created after Waterloo specifically for acts of valour, but was bestowed so freely for other services that it had lost its identity. Appointment to the Bath was in any case restricted to officers of field rank – majors in the Army and naval captains and above. As for campaign medals, those for the Crimea were distributed so casually that many men received them with no more right than the garrison back at Aldershot. Rank and patronage permeated the military awards system at a time when regular army commissions and promotions were purchased rather than earned.

Lord Raglan in the Crimea was soon making so many recommendations for the Bath that the Duke of Newcastle, Secretary-at-War, feared for the Order's integrity. *The Times* thundered against Raglan's dispatch after the battle of Inkerman in November 1854. He had diligently named every general and their entire staffs to the exclusion of the fighting men and their officers.

The Distinguished Conduct Medal for gallantry for sergeants and lower ranks was hastily introduced in December, followed by the Conspicuous Gallantry Medal for naval petty officers and seamen. Though welcome, they failed to address the popular demand for a single supreme award embracing all ranks and all arms. The issue surfaced in the House of Commons on 19 December. Capt George Treweeke Scobell MP, a retired naval officer and Liberal member for Bath, moved 'that an humble address be presented to Her Majesty to institute an "Order of Merit" to be bestowed upon persons serving in the Army or Navy for distinguished and prominent personal gallantry during the present war and to which every grade and individual . . . may be admissible'.

Scobell pointed out that Raglan's soldiers were fighting alongside the French army, which, unlike the British, possessed a gallantry order open to the humblest drummer boy. He withdrew his motion only after government assurances that the matter was already under consideration. Newcastle next consulted the Palace, writing to Prince Albert on 20 January 1855:

Your Royal Highness will recollect that some time ago I expressed an opinion that the circumstances of the present campaign and the alliance in which we have engaged in it seem to render either an extension of the Order of the Bath or the institution of some new Order of Merit, if not necessary, at any rate desirable. . . . Your Royal Highness mentioned several objections to the proposition of adding to the three classes of the Order of the Bath, and . . . I [now] ask Your Royal Highness's opinion upon the other suggestion, the institution of a new decoration to be confined to the Army and the Navy, but open to all ranks of either service. I confess it does not seem to me right or politic that such deeds of heroism as this war has produced should go unrewarded by any distinctive outward mark of honour because they are done by Privates or by Officers below the rank of Major . . .

The value attached by soldiers to a little bit of ribbon is such as to render any danger insignificant and any privation light, if it can be attained, and I believe that great indeed would be the stimulus and deeply prized the reward of a Cross of Military Merit. There are some Orders which even Crowned Heads cannot wear, and it would be a military reward of high estimation if this cross could be so bestowed as to be within the reach of every Private Soldier and yet to be coveted by any General at the head of an Army.

The Duke had raised the subject with Prince Albert before, but clearly nothing had come of it. His letter shows how valueless were the government's assurances to Capt Scobell that the matter was in hand. The Prince replied on the Queen's behalf and at length two days later, strongly approving Newcastle's proposal and suggesting the conditions and form of the award. Victoria favoured 'a small cross of merit for personal deeds of valour, open to all ranks [and] unlimited in number', accompanied by an annual pension of £5. This extremely modest sum was never intended to put a value on the recipient's deed or the decoration. Citing the recent charge of the Light Brigade at Balaclava, whose survivors all deserved the award, Albert pointed out that to decorate every man would reduce the merit of the Cross to the level of a campaign medal. He proposed instead

that in the cases of general actions it be given in certain quantities to particular Regiments, so many to the officers, so many to the sergeants, so many to the men (of the last say 1 per company) and that their distribution be left to a jury of the same rank as the person to be rewarded . . . The limitation of the numbers to be given to a Regiment at one time enforces the *necessity* of a selection and diminishes the pain to those who cannot be included. (Emphasis in original)

Prince Albert ended with an injunction to avoid comparison of the award with the French Legion of Honour, which he dismissed as 'a tool for corruption in the hands of the French Govt . . . which has almost become a necessary appendage to the French dress'. The resulting VC Warrant made provision for ballots. Those conducted for the Crimean War were ad hoc and informal. They were first officially employed during the Indian Mutiny and were last used following the Zeebrugge assault in April 1918. In all, forty-six VCs have been awarded in that way, twenty-nine of them during the Indian Mutiny. Many ballots ignored the strict terms of the Warrant, which became honoured more in the breach than the observance on this issue.

Newcastle informed a restive House of Lords on 29 January that Her Majesty had been advised to institute a 'Cross of Merit' open to all ranks. He lost office next day, when Lord Aberdeen's government fell, unseated by public outrage after revelations of the suffering of the Army in the harsh Crimean winter. Raglan's force was within thirty days of collapse. Of his 25,000 men, 13,000 were sick and 3,000 had died that month alone, most from cholera and dysentery. Some in the frozen trenches were committing suicide. In the field hospitals there was an acute shortage of tentage, medical staff, medicines, beds and bedding, fuel, even rations. Many sick and dying lay crammed and neglected in frozen mud-filled tents or aboard death ships in the harbour. More than one Army doctor broke down. The scandal brought swift reforms.

Credit must go to the Duke of Newcastle for first officially floating the idea of the Cross, but it was Capt Scobell who secured its creation. Newcastle's stewardship at the War Office passed to the dynamic and reforming Lord Panmure – 'the Bison'. His determined views would leave their own mark on the VC. Panmure's difficulty in devising a practical test to be applied to the claims of private soldiers led to nearly a year's delay before a draft was produced setting out the statutes governing the award. Royal approval was sought in December

1855 and the Warrant instituting the VC was signed at Buckingham Palace on 29 January 1856. The nation's supreme and most coveted gallantry award would honour officers and men who 'in the presence of the enemy shall then have performed some signal act of valour or devotion to their country'.

Who actually designed the decoration remains uncertain. The following year the *Illustrated London News* named Mr Charles Hancock, founder of Hancocks & Co., a manufacturing goldsmith and silversmith on the corner of Bruton Street and New Bond Street. The firm had been engaged to make the Cross and remains its sole producer to this day. It is now in the Burlington Arcade. One of Charles Hancock's designers, 27-year-old Henry Armstead, was almost certainly responsible for the detailed design, his style being consistent with that of the Cross. The son of a heraldic chaser, he left Hancocks soon afterwards and eventually became a celebrated sculptor. Sketches of two designs for the Cross and a piece of sheet metal cut to shape had been submitted for royal approval on 3 January. Indicating her choice two days later, the Queen pointed out that the suggested motto 'For the Brave' would imply that non-recipients lacked courage. She decreed 'For Valour'. A proof medal followed on 4 February. The Queen replied the next day:

The Cross looks very well in form but the metal is ugly; it is copper and not bronze and will look very heavy on a red coat with the Crimean ribbon. Bronze is, properly speaking, gun-metal; this has a rich colour and is very hard; copper would wear very ill and would soon look like an old penny. Lord Panmure should have one prepared in real bronze, and the Queen is inclined to think that it ought to have a greenish varnish to protect it; the raised parts would then burnish up bright and show the design and inscription.

This historic first proof is in the Queen's collection at Windsor Castle. The next, in bronze, was returned to Hancock on the 21st with a request for the die to be sunk deeper. The Queen returned two further specimens on 3 March, signifying approval of one of them and asking Hancock for an example 'to keep'. His grandson Col M.P. Hancock presented the approved proof to the Royal United Services Institute Museum in 1922. It is now in the National Army Museum.

A small quasi-Maltese Cross bears the crown and lion of the Royal Crest above a scroll with the words 'For Valour'. The date of the act of gallantry is engraved on the reverse, and details of the recipient on the reverse of the suspender bar, which incorporates an appropriately 'V'-shaped link from which the medal hangs. *The Times* was unimpressed, calling it 'plain and homely, not to say coarse-looking. . . . The whole cross is, after all, poor looking and mean in the extreme.' The unpretentious dignity and simplicity of the design were deliberate, however, contrasting well with the more flashy gallantry medals of some other countries. A red ribbon for the Army and dark blue for the Navy would later become red (actually crimson) for all arms in March 1919 following the creation of the Royal Air Force in April the previous year.

The VC Metal – Myth and Reality

Charles Hancock was instructed on 4 March 1856 to produce the first 106 Victoria Crosses. Medals are normally cast or struck using alloys and cupro-nickels that are easily worked. So hard was the bronze that Hancock received from the War Office that attempts to strike the medal broke his steel dies. He resorted to sand casting. David Callaghan, a past Director of Hancocks, explains the process.

Two iron-framed moulds are filled with sand tightly packed within each frame. The moulds will be mounted one on top of the other in order to produce an object that has both obverse and reverse relief. A casting pattern VC is impressed into each mould, one side producing the obverse and the other the reverse. The molten bronze is then poured into the mould and is directed into the impressions along a central channel. When the metal has cooled the VCs are cut off this central core. Unfortunately the process is wasteful, and any rejects have to be melted down. Because of the nature of the metal much of it cannot be re-used.

Meticulous filing and hand-chasing then follows to highlight the obverse and reverse detail, particularly the lettering and the relief of the central feature of the medal. Finally, a matt bronze patinated finish is applied.

The suspender bars are often cast separately, although they can be cast at the same time as the medal, depending on the size of the moulds used by a particular caster. The suspender bar needs the same hand-finishing as the medal. However, circa 1914 a die was cut for the suspender bar and from then on they were die-struck, minimising the amount of hand finishing required.

Hancock charged the War Office 23*s* (£1.15) per medal complete including ribbon, leather case and engraving. The foundry work continued in-house at what Hancocks habitually called 'the factory' until around 1890. It was subsequently contracted out to Messrs R. Owen Ltd, gold and silver casters, at 25 (later 47) Britton Street, Clerkenwell. For very many years every VC was moulded there by Mr Alec Forbes. He cast his first Cross in around 1915 and celebrated his 750th in 1945. Owens ceased trading in 1963. With the emergence of fraudulent Crosses, a secret mark of authenticity has been added to each one since 1906. The details are known only to Hancocks.

No aspect of the history of the Victoria Cross has been so hotly debated or disputed as the origin of the metal from which it is made. The truth has become fogged by time, myth and misinformation. It all began with a brief report in *The Times* of 2 March 1857 stating that the VC was 'formed from the cannon captured from the Russians'. Though entirely plausible, no official confirmation has ever been found. The idea is attributed to Queen Victoria and certainly typifies her intuitive approach on matters of the Cross. The powerful symbolism is part of its mystique.

VC metal comes today from a pair of muzzle-loading cannon that have stood since at least the 1850s in the Royal Arsenal at Woolwich. However, they are Chinese-made, not Russian. Brig Ken Timbers, chairman of the Royal Artillery Historical Trust, identifies them as approximately 18pdrs, probably coastal defence pieces. How the British Army acquired them remains an impenetrable mystery. Some suggest they were taken by British troops near Canton in the First China Opium War (1839–42). Others believe they were seized in the Crimean War while serving as Russian ordnance, perhaps after capture by the Czar's troops in some Sino-Russian conflict. Each is mounted on a Russian Venglov-pattern iron carriage, which did not necessarily accompany the gun when captured. The barrel's twin stubby projecting bearers or trunnions of one gun have been sleeved to reach the supporting grooves on its carriage. In a letter to *The Times*, 6 November 1985, Deputy Master of the Armouries Mr G.M. Wilson has pointed to the existence in Britain of other Chinese guns on similar carriages that saw service at Sebastopol during the Crimean War.

Part of the myth of the VC is that every Cross has been cast from these two cannon. Some authorities continue to state this as fact, although there is no supporting evidence. Four lines of research, most of it new and hitherto unpublished, disprove the legend and outline the true sequence of events to the present day. The Chinese pieces were not the only, or even the first, to contribute VC metal. An earlier gun provided bronze from the start. When the supply ran out in December 1914, the Chinese cannon took over. Respectively 9ft 4in and 10ft long, they stand today in the Royal Artillery Museum at Woolwich. Each has lost the heavy knoblike cascable projecting from its breech end, around which recoil ropes were secured. The football-size cascabels were sawn off at the neck and melted down for VC production – not in 1856, but nearly sixty years and some 560 Crosses later.

The sequence was signalled in 1993 as two little-known scientific studies neared completion. The Royal Armouries of the Tower of London had used X-ray fluorescence (XRF) spectroscopy to analyse and contrast the metals of the Chinese guns with over seventy VCs, Hancocks' stock, and the mother block held by the Royal Logistic Corps at Donnington. The Australian War Memorial in Canberra conducted a parallel XRF and diffraction study of its fifty-four VCs, and later of fifteen New Zealand-held Crosses. Together they sought to classify VCs by metallic content and date of award. The resultant schedule of 'signatures', unique to each Cross, spans nearly 150 years. Other VCs can now be authenticated or challenged by reference to it. The database has very considerable value and authority in a market where Victoria Crosses are changing hands at up to £235,000.

The studies attracted less Press attention than they deserve because, regrettably, the findings have never been adequately revealed. Twelve years on, the Royal Armouries and the Australian War Memorial (AWM) still have no plans to publish a historical summary. Indeed they cannot, as nearly all the XRF papers have officially gone missing at both institutions.

The AWM first informed the author: 'The research involved testing on Victoria Crosses held both in the Australian War Memorial collection and other hands. Unfortunately the file cannot be copied owing to copyright issues relating to the ownership of some of the medals used in the research.' When asked to explain how copyright could possibly attach to any aspect of the VC, the Memorial replied that, because one or more owners of medals used in the study did not grant, or cannot be contacted to grant, their permission for the release of information pertaining to their medals, the research findings could not be released. The AWM then conceded that some parts were available for viewing, but days later reported that all the XRF papers were found to be missing from the file. We are left to draw our own conclusions as to why neither institution can produce the fruits of its own research. In Wildean terms, to have mislaid one set may be regarded as a misfortune; to lose both looks like – carelessness?

The *Canberra Times* of 5 August 1993 reported: 'The story of the VC analysis [by XRF] came to light when Sotheby's approached the Australian War Memorial to authenticate the VC of Warrant Officer Kevin 'Dasher' Wheatley, which is to go under the hammer in Melbourne on Monday. The Memorial . . . quoted $3500 for an estimated 16 hours work.' The AWM waived the fee on learning that it would be recovered from Wheatley's widow. His VC group (the Cross and seven other medals) sold for A$165,000.

Nevertheless the author has copies of unpublished interim XRF reports from the Armouries and Canberra, and related articles produced by some of the study principals in both countries. They establish beyond all doubt that VCs awarded up to the early months of the First World War were a distinctive copper/tin bronze, deriving from the same basic metal, whereas virtually all the following Crosses come from a very different copper/zinc brass gunmetal. The Armouries study confirms that this later series originates from the Chinese cannon. The findings are supported by a still-unpublished War Office investigation of the origin of the VC metal conducted in 1955 at the urging of Sir Lionel Thompson, Deputy Master of the Royal Mint. The centenary of the Victoria Cross was only weeks away. The Mint was anxious to scotch continuing media speculation concerning its own role in the VC story and to let the public have 'the true facts'. Lt-Gen Sir Colin Callander, the Military Secretary, replied on 30 November:

Although I have not been able to turn up absolute proof, I believe that the Crosses were made from the metal of captured Russian guns. There is a record that in December 1914 the supply of metal in the possession of Messrs Hancocks ran out and was replenished on two occasions by a large piece of metal from guns captured from the Chinese. (TNA PRO: MINT 20/806, WO 32/16088)

Gen Callander left much unsaid, but he pinpoints the timing of the switch to the Woolwich guns. Their Chinese origin was well-known in the War Office and was made public as early as 1916 in the *Illustrated War News*. Two months later, in January 1956, the official catalogue accompanying the VC Centenary Exhibition at Marlborough House cautiously stated that it was 'fairly certain' that VC metal originated from Chinese guns 'during periods in both World Wars'. Ludicrously, a copy of the catalogue placed in the Public Record Office was then embargoed under the '30-year rule'. Its contents were deemed safe for public scrutiny in 1987! (TNA PRO: AIR 20/9847). Close examination of the Woolwich guns has revealed that one indeed bore faint inscriptions in archaic Chinese characters. Prof Dudley Creagh of the Australian XRF team believes their meaning may never be known, telling the *Canberra Times* in 1993 that a copy of the inscriptions was translated in Hong Kong by an expert, 'but the British Army is either being coy about it, or has simply lost the translation'. Further weathering has rendered the inscriptions almost illegible. The guns are now under cover. More than once Creagh and his researchers ran up against the veil of tradition and mystique surrounding the Victoria Cross, meeting with silence from certain informed sources in London and Australia.

The Chinese cannon could not have serviced Hancocks much before 1914 in any case without losing a lot more metal. Mark Smith, curator of the Royal Artillery Museum, confirms they have shed only their cascabels, whose combined weight he estimates to be some 224lb. This squares with the author's independent research, which concluded that approximately

220lb of metal would have been needed to cast the 810 VCs gazetted since December 1914 plus the residual block at Donnington and allowance for Hancocks' stock. VC metal consumption can be calculated with fair accuracy. Every twelve finished Crosses together weigh only 10–11oz, but require an average melt of 47oz of gunmetal. The high wastage arises because sometimes two in every three medals cast are rejected as imperfect. The discards and the 'casting tree', the solidified run of the pouring that links the moulds, usually six at a time, are normally scrapped as being too disturbed for re-melting. (The VC Registers at The National Archives record production orders to Hancocks between 1856 and 1908, and the weights and dates of bronze supplied. The average metal consumption rate is calculated from this and is supported by later records.)

As for the very first VC bronze, XRF analysis indicates that it originated from a common basic source, almost certainly a single cannon. By the time the supply ran out near the end of 1914 it must have contributed close to 140lb for some 560 Crosses, including a handful of reissues. Nothing more is known, save its metallic make-up and the *Times* report of its Crimean War origin. Its provenance will surely become the focus of future research.

Hancocks' prestigious VC work was threatened in 1923 when the Royal Mint attempted to take it over. In a bullish letter to the War Office on 3 January the Deputy Master expressed his 'surprise and consternation that the private firm of Jewellers who make the VCs for the Army Council rook them to the extent of charging £1.11.6 [£1.57] for each decoration'. He quoted 11s 6d (57.5p), failing to realise that the Crosses were not struck but expensively cast and finished. Receiving no encouragement from the military, the Mint withdrew.

Attempts were made to dismiss reports that the supply of 'Crimean' VC gunmetal had run out during the Second World War. The War Office ensured that little further information escaped its net, and with the passage of time the drama has degraded to little more than rumour. To general dismay, the flow of metal was reported to have ceased early in 1942. The BBC broke the news on 16 March in an 8.00 a.m. bulletin, announcing that the supply was exhausted and that arrangements had been made for provision from another source. *The Times* contacted Hancocks, reporting the next day: 'Victoria Crosses are being made from a new supply of bronze as the original supply has been used. A director of the London jewellers who fashion and inscribe the crosses said yesterday that . . . the supply of the Sebastopol metal had run out. In future the Maltese crosses will be made from a gunmetal supplied by the Mint.'

In reportedly confirming the news and naming the Mint as supplier, Hancocks added to rising alarm at the War Office, which was caught unawares. Concern centred on finding the source of the story, and a means of defusing the issue in the face of evident public anxiety. Explanations were sought by the Military Secretary, Lt-Gen Floyer-Ackland. The BBC brazenly claimed that it had taken the news from the *Times* report – rightly gauging that nobody was likely to remember that the broadcast had gone out early on the day before the paper's appearance. Director W.H.J. 'Jimmy' Wixley at Hancocks declared that its three directors had never gone beyond telling enquirers that after the original Crimea gunmetal had become exhausted in the First World War, all subsequent Crosses had originated from part of another gun supplied by the War Office. The Mint's Deputy Master responded that it was not concerned with manufacture of the VC, and Hancocks had just informed him that they had neither run out of metal nor knew where it came from. In an opaque reference to its Chinese origin, he suggested that 'there may be no advantage at the present moment in enlightening the public as to which, if any, of the United Nations is now supplying, albeit involuntarily, metal for the Cross'. The Military Secretary agreed.

The Victoria Cross is administered today by MS1, an inter-services department of the Military Secretary's office at the Ministry of Defence. In 1942 it was designated MS3, its responsibilities including the ordering of Crosses from Hancocks and of VC metal from the newly appointed Ministry of Supply. The Ministry was solely responsible for procurement and storage of the metal. MS3 remained historically distanced from this aspect. It kept no coherent record of the metal's origin, location, and periodic issues and balances. Therein lay the core of the confusion. In truth, the metal had gone missing.

The news brought immediate offers of captured Crimean cannon from public parks all over the country. Shaftesbury's Borough Surveyor got his in first, writing on the day of the broadcast. Three weeks later the War Office response was agreed, Brig W.A. Turner, its Deputy Director of Public Relations (DDPR), minuting MS3 on 4 May:

> I suggest we reply on the following lines, with appropriate 'trimmings'.

> 'It is true that the BBC announcement was couched in terms which could be misinterpreted. The facts are that the supply of metal from the original bronze Crimean gun from which the earlier Victoria Crosses were cast, has been exhausted, and another piece of artillery captured in action has been supplied to take the place of the original. There was no intention of conveying the idea that artillery relics from the Crimea have gone out of existence in this country, because such is not the case.' (TNA: PRO WO 32/16088)

Having charged the BBC with imprecision, the DDPR does little better. The run-out to which he refers arose not in the present war but in 1914, yet his vagueness leaves the impression that it occurred recently and thus tied in with the BBC and *Times* reports. Brig Turner believed them to be garbled versions of Hancock's statement and felt it a waste of time to probe further. The hiatus ran on for a full year, when Donnington's commandant minuted the War Office in March 1943:

It has been reported by the officer in charge, Field Stores, Donnington that he is holding 53lbs of [VC gunmetal] in stock. This officer states that he has seen a remark in the Press that no more of this metal was available, and the stock referred to above is brought to your notice in case it has been overlooked that some of this metal is still held by Ordnance. (TNA: PRO WO 32/21740)

The War Office contacted Hancocks and was told that they held little metal. Donnington was ordered to dispatch 25lb. The crisis was over and the original VC supply was restored. This was formally confirmed in an Ordnance Department memo in May 1948 from Lt-Col Horton at Donnington. He reported that the mother block was known to have lain at Woolwich Arsenal since at least 1924. His records showed that it was transferred to Donnington during the war when part of the Arsenal was evacuated, and the present metal was the self-same block (TNA: PRO WO 32/16088). This disproves stories that the block was destroyed by enemy bombing at Woolwich, though the Luftwaffe certainly accelerated its transfer.

The War Office was compelled to remain silent to avoid presenting Germany with a propaganda coup. Rumour and media confusion ensued until 1956, the centenary year of the Victoria Cross. The Press in its ignorance had continued, unchallenged, to name the Mint as Hancocks' supplier. Typical of the public's undiminished concern was a letter received by the War Office in 1952 from Mr R.A. Porritt, a gardener with the Middlesbrough Parks Department, who reported spotting a Russian cannon from the Crimean War bearing the imperial double-headed eagle, which lay forgotten in Stewart's Park, Marton.

Despite official evasions at the time and the inevitable combing of files before later release, there remains clear evidence of an inadvertent but serious gunmetal stoppage. It is supported by the sudden appearance of a VC metal in 1942–3 that differs markedly in composition from any previous or later issue. Its coincidental emergence during the stoppage suggests it can only have been an emergency batch on the initiative of the Ministry of Supply.

These indications first surfaced in 1956, when the Royal Mint finally denied ever having produced VC metal. There is no documented reason to doubt this, despite the Mint's previously evasive responses to all who wrote seeking a straightforward 'yes or no'. Sir Lionel Thompson also got around to challenging *Whitakers Almanack*, which for years, with other reference works, had been naming the Mint as Hancocks' supplier. The editor replied on 27 January that the War Office had already raised the matter with him, adding:

> The Secretary of the Battle Honours Committee [Brig-Gen R.G. Thurburn] mentioned that the Ministry of Supply took over the supply of the metal from 1942. He established during his own researches that Chinese gunmetal was used for the Crosses in 1914, and informed us that 'There is no firm confirmation that Crimean gunmetal was being used again [i.e. from 1942] until 1948, since when ample stocks have been available for the manufacture of Crosses.' (TNA: PRO MINT 20/806)

Gen Thurburn's readiness to concede that non-Crimean gunmetal may have been used to make VCs between 1942 and 1948 is notable, as also his reference to the appointment of the Ministry of Supply. He had only just concluded the search of War Office archives for the history of VC metal, reporting on 13 December 1955:

> MS3 have file references to show that Crimean gunmetal was in use again, at least, in April 1948. It is reasonable to suppose that Sir Cuthbert Whittaker would not have inserted the statement in [*Whittaker's Almanac*] without good authority. Moreover, in wartime conditions it is very

likely that the Ministry of Supply, who were not ordinarily concerned with gunmetal for VCs, might not have found it easy to locate the correct stocks. It is therefore probable that both stoppages of the correct gunmetal, which occurred during the First and Second World Wars, were due to war-time conditions when normal supplies were dislocated. (TNA: PRO WO 32/16088)

Gen Thurburn's unequivocal reference to a gunmetal stoppage in the Second World War, together with his other revelations, confirm its occurrence. As he suggests, the wartime transfer of the VC block from Woolwich Arsenal with tens of thousands of stores to dispersed depots may indeed have rendered it impossible to trace.

Additionally, the Australian XRF studies recorded a change in the composition of VC metal in 1942–3. Team leader Dr John Ashton, Senior Conservator at the AWM, identifies five Crosses awarded between 1942 and 1945 whose metallic composition is a high-copper bronze, quite unlike the copper/zinc brass of the Chinese or any other series. Among these bronze issues is the Cross held by the New Zealander Capt Charles Hazlitt Upham VC and Bar, which Dr Ashton relates to others of similar composition from 1943. Some confusion surrounds the three VCs that were produced for Charles Upham's initial act. It arose through his capture before the first could be presented, and the subsequent engraving of a replacement Cross on his release, which he received from the King in May 1945. He was then gazetted in September for the Bar, causing London to commission yet a third Cross bearing the dates of both acts. Suffice to say that Upham declined it, preferring to retain the Cross received at the King's hands. This bronze decoration must have come from Hancocks' unique 1942–3 stock, whereas the Bar struck in 1945 matches the Chinese gunmetal.

The discovery was reported by Dr Ashton in his important but largely overlooked article 'The Analysis of Victoria Crosses in New Zealand', published by the Anzac Fellowship in 1995. He was struck by the anomaly and could offer no reason for it, clearly having little knowledge of the background and the supply break. The British study may well have identified other such Crosses. This is but one example of the current situation, which is preventing a full historical interpretation of the 'missing' XRF data in both countries. Dr Ashton's excellent but limited report is the most informative of the few that touch on the XRF work. The findings cannot be allowed to become private property. Certain details of individual VCs must naturally remain undisclosed to prevent duplication leading to forgery of missing Crosses, but the sponsoring public institutions in both countries should get a grip of this material and permit detailed study of its historical implications.

The War Office unearthed an old box in April 1946 containing seven engraved bronze VCs cast in the 1800s. They appeared to be duplicates, and came to light when MS3 was packing for an office move. All seven were to be sent to Hancocks for removal of engraving, restoring and rebronzing before going into stock, but Hancocks' invoice for the work covered only six. By June 1951 five of them were no longer on Hancocks' inventory. Again, the XRF findings may tell us more.

The mother ingot of VC gunmetal, stock item M3/9680999644816, is locked in its own container in a vault in the Small Arms Building at the Central Ordnance Depot of the Royal Logistic Corps, Donnington. Alone among the 350,000 items on inventory, it is priceless. Whenever removed, it must always be under guard with an officer present. At just over 22lb (358oz) the block is good for up to ninety more Crosses. XRF analysis confirms that it originates from the less heavily hooped of the two cannon at Woolwich. Some 360lb have been taken from all sources to produce the 1,351 VCs and 3 Bars that had been awarded at the time this book went to press, plus the Cross to the American Unknown Soldier of the First World War, replacement VCs and the residual metal.

Because they are cast and chased, no two Victoria Crosses are exactly the same. It seems fitting that each uniquely gallant act should be honoured by a decoration that itself remains unique.

The Netley Casket, 1966

A touching discovery followed the lifting of the foundation stone of an abandoned military hospital on 7 December 1966. It had been built at Queen Victoria's urging during the outcry over medical services in the Crimea. She had laid the Welsh granite block at Netley's vast Royal Victoria Hospital overlooking Southampton Water on 19 May 1856. A copper casket was placed beneath it, *The Times* enigmatically reporting that the Queen had deposited therein 'coins, medals and cross and the vellum document regarding the event'. But what 'cross'? Intense speculation accompanied preparations to raise the one-ton stone more than a century later. Col Desmond Murphy, the commandant, laid on a grand ceremony attended by VIPs, TV cameras and a large crowd on the muddy site. Fearful of an anticlimax, he and his RSM sneaked a preview the night before. They opened the casket to find among much else a Crimea medal with four clasps and a 'blank' Victoria Cross.

The Queen had acknowledged receipt of a Cross from Hancock only a fortnight before the stone-laying. He was busy producing the first 106 VCs, of which the Netley Cross must be one. The example requested by the Queen in March was specifically 'to keep'. The Netley Cross is held today in the Army Medical Services Museum at Keogh Barracks, Mytchett, near Aldershot. It was engraved in 1967 to establish its identity. Details of the inscription are kept secret.

The Victoria Cross Annuity

A special annual annuity of £10 was payable to non-commissioned holders of the VC, with a further £5 for each Bar. It was intended to provide a few personal comforts and was never meant to reflect the value of the award in monetary terms. It remained unchanged for over 100 years, despite growing parliamentary criticism. Discretionary powers were granted in 1898 to increase the amount to a means-tested limit of £50 in cases where VC recipients 'from old age or infirmity not due to their own fault, may be in poor circumstances'. Officers could also seek this allowance, which rose to £75 in 1921. A particularly mean condition of entry to the Royal Hospital as a Chelsea Pensioner required holders of the Cross to forgo their VC annuity. Organisers of a commemorative dinner in 1929 for Victoria Cross veterans had to raise funds to buy clothes and provide free transport and accommodation for 'a considerable number' of their honoured guests.

In 1943 Lady Apsley MP raised cheers in the Commons when she called for the standard VC annuity to be increased to £100 tax free. Clement Attlee, Secretary of State for the Dominions, coolly replied for the government that the original £10 appeared adequate and 'there have been no particular complaints about this'. As Prime Minister in 1947 he remained immovable, though by then the sum had been supplemented by an extra 6d (2.5p) per day on the holder's service pension. At the urging of Brig Sir John Smyth VC MP, the £10 rate was at last increased to £100 tax free in 1959, and became payable to officers for the first time. The little-claimed hardship allowance was abolished. The annuity was increased to £1,300 in 1995, at which time there were thirty-three living recipients. It is £1,495 at the time of writing.

The First Investiture, 26 June 1857

Formal selection for the VC began in January 1857 only after the delay had been criticised in the House by the dogged Capt Scobell, and later by the Queen. Strict observance of ballot procedures under the Warrant so long after the event would have stalled the process, but a few regimental commanders had conducted informal ballots among their men at the time.

Recommendations for 112 VCs were submitted to the Queen. One name was struck off at her request. Pte P M'Gwire of the 33rd was captured by two Russian soldiers while on advanced sentry duty. He waited his opportunity before grabbing his own gun from one and shooting the other. The first sentry fired at him and missed before M'Gwire brained him with a blow from the butt. Draped with the accoutrements of his victims, he was fired at by Russian outpost sentries before reaching his own lines to the cheers of fellow pickets. Queen Victoria considered his action of doubtful morality. If approved, it would signal the advisability of shooting future prisoners. M'Gwire was nevertheless rewarded by Lord Raglan and received the French Médaille Militaire.

The Queen invested 62 of the 111 Crimea recipients at a parade in London's Hyde Park on a brilliantly hot Friday 26 June 1857. Eager crowds headed for the sound of bands on the old parade ground flanking Park Lane, where 9,000 men of all arms awaited their sovereign, the peppery Gen Sir Colin Campbell at their head. Thousands of parasols behind the barriers and on the stands were soon unfurling in the sunshine. Cheering greeted the men about to receive the Cross as they marched on in single file at 9.45, halting in front of a central pavilion between two grandstands, from where veteran Chelsea Pensioners eyed them intently. The line was headed by the Senior Service – a naval party of twelve followed by regimental groupings, a Grenadier Guards colonel standing behind an RE Sapper, a Coldstream Brevet major behind a guardsman. Some were newly retired. George Walters in police uniform had recently been a sergeant of the 49th. He had bravely rescued Gen Adams at Inkerman, bayoneting one of his assailants. Now he was a constable on 18s a week. Bearded ex-Cpl Robert Shields of the 23rd wore a park-keeper's green livery. He had volunteered to make his way through murderous fire to bring in wounded Lt Dyneley. By some miracle he achieved this, but poor Dyneley was declared dead.

A 21-gun salute preceded the arrival of the royal procession at the old Hyde Park Corner gate at 10.00 sharp. The Queen in a suitably military ensemble rode Sunset, her favourite charger, Prince Albert at her side. To general surprise she declined the dais. Sitting her horse, she took position in front of the pavilion beside a scarlet-draped table bearing sixty-two Crosses.

A loop had hastily been sewn above every man's left breast shortly before the investiture when it was realised that the Queen could not be expected to pin through heavy serge. Cdr Henry James Raby of the Naval Brigade was first to receive the Cross. It was rumoured, perhaps falsely, that he manfully stood unflinching as the royal aim missed the loop and pinned the medal directly into his chest. Lt Charles Lucas RN, first to win the Cross, was fourth in line by rank, and behind him Lt William Hewett, whose defiance in refusing to spike his Lancaster had so impressed the Queen that her diary records her pleasure in decorating him that morning. The first Army recipient was Sgt-Maj John Grieve, who had so mightily laid about him with his cavalry sabre at Balaclava.

The simple presentation was over in ten minutes. Many spectators on the distant far side remained unaware that it had taken place. Some of the 7,000 guests in the stands flanking the royal pavilion fared little better. Only those at the front had the angle of vision, while all suffered the effects on feet and ankles of a steeply ramped deck lacking seats and stepped terraces. The organisation of the whole event, the largest military ceremonial ever staged in London until then, was nevertheless a triumph of short-order staff work. The Queen had given the War Office just twelve days' notice to stage it, perhaps mindful that the announcement of her beloved Albert's new title as Prince Consort was to be made that same day. The lists of names to be engraved reached Charles Hancock only seven days before the parade.

The proud holders re-formed in line to face the royal party before Campbell led the parade in immaculate review between them. The 11th Hussars thundered heart-stoppingly past, some

Balaclava chargers among them and with Lord Cardigan at their head on Ronald, the horse that had carried him that immortal morning. They drew special cheers and not a few tears from the 100,000 spectators reportedly present. (Ronald lived on to take part in Cardigan's funeral procession in 1868. *The Times* reports that the old charger was well sedated by laudanum to calm his thoroughbred nerves, becoming excited only when a bugler sounded the charge. He is now stabled in a glass case under the main stairs at the family seat, Deene Park, Northamptonshire.) The parade in all its colour ended at 11.45 with three hearty cheers for the Queen. She had opened, as *The Times* rightly observed, a new epoch in Britain's military history.

3

The Indian Mutiny, 1857–1859

I know not what course events may take. . . . We must
not forget that in the sky of India, serene as it is, a
small cloud may arise, at first no bigger than a man's
hand, but which growing bigger and bigger, may at
last threaten to overwhelm us with ruin.

*(Lord Canning, on taking oath of office
as Governor-General of India, 1 August 1855)*

It is unfashionable to acknowledge that Britain was once the
most powerful nation on earth. Its colonisation, sometimes
fiercely imposed, sought trade not conquest. The Victorians
additionally believed it a moral duty to replace cruel barbarism
with Christianity. For most of the nineteenth century Britain's
domination of world trade was underpinned by the still-growing
empire, of which India was the 'Jewel in the Crown'. Less than
100,000 British soldiers and administrators held dominion over
India's 250 million peoples.

After the costly victories of the Crimea, the Army returned to
imperial duties. In India it met bloody rebellion. Only 26,000 of
Victoria's troops were garrisoned there. They were known as
'Queen's regiments' to distinguish them from those solely in the
pay of the Honourable East India Company, which had 15,000
European infantry under command, and 233,000 native troops
(sepoys) officered by Europeans. Much of Britain's entire
military strength was owned and substantially controlled by the
Company, which was established by Royal Charter in 1600 to
acquire territory and raise armies against native rulers. By the
mid-1800s the unsettling pace of change increased native fears

of a move to impose Christianity by stealth. Unrest spread beneath surface calm like firedamp in a mine.

The explosion came from disaffected sepoys with no incentive but their pay to keep them loyal. The waterproofed cartridge for the new Enfield rifle was a sealed and greased paper tube. Its end had to be bitten off and the contents poured down the barrel before the following ball was rammed home. Agitators alleged the grease that would touch their lips was deliberately made from beef and pork fat, abominations to Hindus and Muslims alike. Thus defiled, it was said, they would be driven to accept Christianity. The authorities hastily ordered that the wrapper should be torn off by hand. Issue of a vegetable-oil grease followed, enabling sepoys to treat their own ungreased cartridges. Eighty-five sowars (troopers) of the 3rd Bengal Light Cavalry at Meerut near Delhi refused to accept them. They were court-martialled, paraded and disgraced before imprisonment. The whole garrison mutinied next day, 10 May 1857. British officers were cut down and many of their wives suffered horrific violation before death with their children.

Maddened with bhang, the mutineers made for Delhi to be joined by the Indian garrison in frenzied looting, arson, rape and murder. The rebellion spread quickly but unevenly through the State of Oudh and its capital Lucknow, and on into Bengal and Central India. More than half the Bengal army mutinied, though in the other commands only two regiments joined them. It became a civil war in which thousands of Indians fought loyally beside the British, but the Company lost control of a huge area. Authority was restored after fourteen months of barbarism on both sides, as well as notable instances of high courage. The government of India passed from the Company to the Crown in 1858. Its great army was disbanded two years later, to be replaced by the British-administered Indian Army.

The Indian Mutiny produced 182 VCs, the same number as awarded for the entire Second World War. Many of the acts of great heroism that earned the Cross in the 1800s would have gained a lesser decoration in later years when alternatives were introduced.

The Red Fort Magazine, Delhi, 11 May 1857

Lt George Forrest. Lt William Raynor. Conductor John Buckley

As Delhi burned that morning, a strong body of mutineers stormed the granite-walled Red Fort housing Upper India's largest magazine of powder and arms. The Fort's nine British officers and NCOs led by Lt George Willoughby of the Bengal Artillery determined to defend it to the death, and to blow the main magazine when they were overwhelmed. His two 6pdrs were double-charged with grapeshot and trained on the barricaded outer gate. A huge 74pdr commanded the inner courtyard, where a powder train was laid from a lime tree to the main explosives stores. When the mutineers' demand for surrender was refused, they swarmed scaling ladders against the outer walls. All the Fort's native defenders including the gun-lascars and artificers deserted to the mob. For five long hours under the furnace heat of an Indian sun the handful of defenders poured shot into repeated attacks at the gate and from the walls. By mid-afternoon all ready ammunition was exhausted. Rebels were infiltrating the Fort. No defender could reach the magazine and expect to return. Willoughby signalled Conductor John Scully to fire the train.

An eye-searing flash leapt from the tree and across the yard into the magazine, which erupted, detonating scores of cartridge barrels half-sunk into the ground whose shot merged with heavy munitions hurling shrapnel, masonry and shredded timber into the mutineers. The 40ft walls of the inner keep collapsed outwards onto them. A thousand were thought to have died in the explosions, which were heard 34 miles away at Meerut. Amazingly, several defenders survived, though all were more or less injured. Lts William Raynor and George Forrest of the

Bengal Veteran Establishment, and Conductor John Buckley of the Army's Commissariat Department, reached Meerut, together with Raynor's wife and child, who had sheltered inside the Fort. The three men received the Cross for their most gallant conduct. Raynor, aged 61 and 10 months, is believed to be the oldest ever to gain the VC. George Willoughby became separated and was killed. He richly deserved the award, as did Scully at the train, for he knew that he must die when he fired it. Dead heroes would be denied posthumous VCs for another 45 years.

Cawnpore, June–July 1857

Lt Henry Marsham Havelock

The horrors of Cawnpore's siege profoundly affected all British and many Indian soldiers. The native garrison had deserted. Many of the remaining 300 European troops were sick. They and the rest of the white community assembled in a compound hastily thrown up beside the Ganges, hoping for early rescue by river. On 6 June the mutineers began an artillery bombardment of the crowded and exposed site. It continued intermittently for twenty days. The suffering of all, including several hundred women and children, was indescribable. The garrison commander surrendered on a rebel pledge of safe passage down river to Allahabad. Instead, the packed barges were raked with grape and ball in a treacherous massacre as they departed. No man who struggled ashore was spared, but some 250 women and children were hauled out alive, only to be butchered with swords and meat cleavers on 15 July following news of Brig-Gen Sir Henry Havelock's avenging relief column, 'coming like mad dogs'. The column reached the slaughterhouse the next day, where a sickened Lt North recorded 'the clotted gore lay ankle deep'. Many of the dead and dying were thrown down a well nearby. The barbarity at Cawnpore followed an appalling massacre of over 6,000 Indians in Allahabad by European Company troops led by Col James Neill.

Gen Havelock's 2,000 soldiers had to beat off an estimated 13,000 rebels to reach Cawnpore. Having captured seven guns at the point of the bayonet on the 16th, the exhausted 64th Regiment was halted by mutineers rallying on a reserve 24pdr. Havelock ordered them to storm it. His newly appointed ADC, his son Henry Marsham Havelock, spurred ahead unbidden to find the battalion lying down in line before the gun. Seeing no mounted officers, the Lieutenant called the men up and rode on towards the cannon at a measured walk regardless of a hot fire, much of which was directed on him. The men took the gun in a final rush, watched by Maj Stirling, their much discomfited commander, who was on foot, his horse having been shot under him before Havelock's arrival. Unseen by Lt Havelock, Stirling suffered the indignity of a junior staff officer usurping his command and leading his men to capture a gun. The Regiment was further incensed when Sir Henry provisionally conferred the Cross on his own son, whose integrity and courage were never in question. Indeed, he had tried to dissuade his father. His later exploits caused Lord Wolseley to name him 'the bravest man in the British Army'. Havelock's VC was gazetted in January 1858.

Young Havelock might have become the first to gain a Bar to the VC, but delays in communication with London and increased suspicion of nepotism conspired against him. As his father's relief column neared besieged Lucknow in September 1857 it met furious resistance at the Char-Bhag bridge. Lt Havelock, highly conspicuous as the only mounted soldier, led the Madras Fusiliers in an assault through heavy and sustained rebel fire from rooftops and artillery on the far side. When the bridge had been stormed and the guns taken, the smoke cleared to reveal Havelock calmly sitting his horse and waving the following troops on. He was almost the sole survivor of the attacking party, unscathed save for a bullet through his helmet. Lt-Gen Sir James Outram recommended him for a Bar, which Brig-Gen Havelock once again provisionally conferred on his son. This was untrodden ground. Mindful of the sensitivities surrounding the Lieutenant's first award, the War Office referred the submission back to the fiery Sir Colin Campbell, now C-in-C India, for comment. Campbell, who had little time for the VC, assembled a Board of Field Officers, which concluded that a Bar should not be awarded, 'as it was not known in this country [India] at the time the [second] recommendation was made that the decoration had already been conferred in England for another service'. The War Office rightly condemned that logic as irrational. Each recommendation related to a different exploit. An award for one should not influence consideration of the other. India, displeased with Gen Havelock's perceived nepotism, was clearly prepared to sanction only one VC for the price of two. The War Office reluctantly concurred. In fact, since Havelock's VC had not been gazetted at the time of the second recommendation on 17 October 1857, he held no Cross and the question of a Bar did not arise.

Award to Indian Services and Civilians

Mr Ross L. Mangles. Mr William McDonell

Soldiers of the Company who fought shoulder to shoulder with the British Army were ineligible for the VC. A Warrant to include 'the officers and men of the naval and military service of the East India Company' received royal assent in October 1857. Although this form of words did not discriminate between native and European officers and men, the Company objected that the former already had the Indian Order of Merit. It had been instituted for gallantry in 1837 and pre-dated any British Army gallantry medal. The Company pointed out it would be wrong for native troops to benefit from two such decorations when the British Army had only the one. The War Office agreed. The embargo continued until 1911 when a Warrant extended award of the VC to Indian officers and men of the Indian Army. It was surely not by chance that this coincided with the King-Emperor's departure for Delhi for the Coronation Durbar.

The ferocity of the Mutiny caused most European men and not a few boys to bear arms alongside the soldiers during heavy fighting. It followed that they too should become eligible for the Cross. A Warrant in December 1858 extended the VC to all civilians who bore arms while under the orders of an officer in command of troops. Ross Lewis Mangles, a 24-year-old Patna assistant magistrate, was one of four civilians to gain VCs during the Mutiny. He volunteered to join a column that was dispatched to relieve Arrah in Behar Province in July 1857. The force was ambushed on the night of the 29th. During the retreat next day under a blazing sun and murderous rebel fire from concealment along the route, the already wounded Mangles carried a soldier of the 37th for an agonising 6 miles across semi-swamp to a waiting boat. Both survived, but the column lost 300 of its 450 men.

Mr William McDonell of the Bengal Civil Service was another, earning his Cross as a volunteer guide in that same retreat. The survivors had reached the boats in disorder, only to find that the rebels had removed the oars and lashed the tillers fast. Many fell under a storm of fire as they thrashed about trying to drag heavy boats into the water and hack through the restraining ropes. McDonell, already wounded and with a stiffening limb, calmly rallied the survivors and joined the last boat after helping others aboard. The thirty-five white Company soldiers crouching on the bottom boards ignored his shouts to cut the lashings, so he climbed onto the thatched roof above the rudder in a storm of bullets and did the job himself, as two balls passed through his hat. He too survived.

Lucknow, June–November 1857

Pte Henry Ward. Pte Tom Duffy. Mr Thomas Kavanagh. AB William Hall RN. Lt Thomas Young RN. Lt Nowell Salmon RN. LS John Harrison RN. Lt Robert Aitken

If the intensity of the conflict was to be measured by the numbers of Crosses awarded, then Lucknow, with nearly sixty, was certainly the most hard won. The capital was besieged from 30 June until 17 November, with a break of only a few hours in September. The British community of some 800, including over 500 women and children, took refuge with others in the hastily fortified Residency and grounds with Sir Henry Lawrence the Governor. The garrison comprised one British regiment, the 32nd Foot, and four loyal native units. Sir Henry was killed on the second day of the siege when a shell burst in his bedroom. Daily shelling, death and injury were met with inspiring fortitude among all in the compound, British and Indian.

The first relief column was led by Gens Sir Henry Havelock and Sir James Outram. It suffered heavy losses and gained thirteen VCs before reaching the compound on 26 September. The weakened column had no option but to remain with the defenders. Young Lt Henry Havelock had sustained a smashed elbow when his horse was shot under him the previous evening. Pte Henry Ward of the 78th The Seaforth Highlanders remained beside the unconscious officer throughout the night before leading stretcher parties carrying Havelock and an injured Highlander through much fire to safety. Ward received the Cross and was later promoted Quartermaster Sergeant.

Attempts were made on the 26th to recover a 24pdr gun lost overnight. Its exposed position was under rebel fire, but Pte Tom Duffy of the 1st Madras Fusiliers and Artillerymen Olpherts and Crump volunteered to retrieve it. In a display of raw courage and ingenuity 52-year-old Duffy managed to secure a rope to the gun's trail as musket balls struck the ground around him. The precious gun was dragged to safety and immediately deployed to clear a passage through palace grounds, enabling the rest of the ordnance to reach the Residency. Duffy's fine exploit ensured the safe arrival of every gun and ammunition wagon. His prized VC was sold in London in 1902 for £53.

Thomas Kavanagh of the Indian civil service was the third civilian to earn a well-deserved VC. His wife Agnes and four of their fourteen children had gone to stay with friends in Cawnpore for the summer. They escaped the massacres there when a disagreement with their hosts brought them back early to Lucknow. Agnes was wounded in the shelling there and lost her baby. In November a second relief column approached with over 2,000 men led by Sir Colin Campbell. Kavanagh, a tall bearded 36-year-old, offered to cross enemy lines and guide it in. Disguised as a rebel soldier, he slipped out of the Residency after dark on 9 November with Kunoujee Lal, a trusted Brahman spy who would guide him to Campbell's camp 15 miles off at Alum Bagh. The big Irishman carried a double-barrelled pistol ready loaded, not for defence but to ensure his own death and that of his guide before rebels could lay hands on them. They were stopped many times, on some occasions waved on, on others having to run for their lives. They reached the British camp just before dawn in a state of collapse, having lost their way and waded waist deep through a swamp for two hours. A signal was semaphored to inform the Residency of their safe arrival. It was only then that Agnes was told of her husband's mission. He guided the advance on the city, witnessing on the way the slaughter of 2,000 rebels, bayoneted by British and Sikh troops avenging Cawnpore. The fourth civilian VC of the Mutiny was gained on 27 September 1858 by A/Master George B. Chicken, a volunteer with the Indian Naval Brigade.

Campbell's column included a naval brigade of heavy guns led by the charismatic Capt William Peel VC, who had won his Cross at Inkerman. Four of his gunners gained VCs on 16 November when attempting to breach the 20ft walls of Lucknow's heavily defended Shah Najaff mosque. The six crews ran their 24pdrs close up to the wall beneath a punishing sepoy cross-fire and blazed away with roundshot for three hours, losing many men and making no impression. At dusk, in a desperate last attempt, Peel ordered two guns right forward to maximise penetrating power. When most of the crew of one gun fell, AS William Hall from Nova Scotia, *Shannon*'s coloured

Captain of the Foretop, raced across to support battery officer Lt Thomas Young on the gun. Three more sailors joined them. After each round they ran the 2.5-ton piece closer until they were in mortal danger from flying stone fragments. When the other gun's crew was wiped out, and Hall alone remained at his, he continued to serve it single-handedly, doing the work of four men until rejoined by a badly wounded Lt Young. The semi-fortress was finally taken when its defenders, unnerved by the gunners' determination, withdrew that evening.

Peel's men had been taking casualties earlier from a sniper high in the wall whose position was overlooked by a tree. Several attempts to climb its branches proved fatal before Lt Nowell Salmon succeeded, killing the sepoy. LS John Harrison then joined him, passing up loaded rifles as Salmon picked off more rebels until he was shot and severely wounded. Harrison then took over and continued the work to good effect.

AB Hall, Lt Young, Lt Salmon and LS Harrison received VCs. William Hall, powerfully built and a fine runner, was the first coloured man to be awarded the Cross. He became a petty officer before retirement to his home in Canada, where he died in 1904. Lt Young's brother-in-law Midshipman Duncan Boyes also gained the Cross, in Japan in 1864. Nowell Salmon ended his service as Admiral of the Fleet. Capt Peel was appointed Knight Commander of the Bath for his gallant leadership. He died of fever the following April.

So desperate was the fighting that twenty-three VCs were earned in Lucknow on this one day, 16 November. A twenty-fourth Cross was won in distant Narnoul by Lt Francis Brown of the 1st European Bengal Fusiliers. Unsurprisingly, the record remains unbroken. Campbell entered the Residency next day and evacuated the garrison, returning the refugees to Cawnpore and leaving behind a holding force to await his return in greater strength. The exceptionally bloody recapture of Lucknow followed in March 1858, though many thousands of rebels escaped with their leaders through the inept handling of the assault by Campbell and a cavalry commander. Of those who were captured, 40 sepoys were tied to the mouths of cannon and blown from the guns, while 2,000 more were bayoneted to death in the Secundra Bagh to British shouts of 'Remember Cawnpore!'

The most bizarre of any VC award ceremony must be that of Lt Robert H.M. Aitken, a member of the 13th Bengal Native Infantry. His deeds at Lucknow were so numerous that his citation spans the entire period of the siege. A general parade was subsequently ordered beside the ruins of the Residency at which Sir Hugh Rose the C-in-C was to present the decoration. All the great and good of Lucknow were invited. On the morning, as the parade was drawing up, it was discovered that Aitken's VC had been left behind in Simla in the Himalayas. This rather awkward situation was bound to infuriate Sir Hugh. What to do? The nearest officer possessing a Cross was at Cawnpore, hours away. Minutes before the ceremony Col Donald Stewart the Deputy Adjutant General bravely volunteered to tell the C-in-C. The resulting explosion was possibly audible to the parade, but the resourceful Stewart then proposed a cunning plan to which Sir Hugh readily agreed. The ceremony passed off with great success, the C-in-C pinning the cross of the Companionship of the Bath to Aitken's breast. Stewart reclaimed it that evening before the ball in honour of the occasion, at which Aitken's dancing partners were mildly surprised to notice that his Cross was a piece of painted leather.

Siege of Delhi, June–September 1857, and the VC Ballot

Lt Alfred Heathcote. Pte James Thompson. Pte John Divane. Bugler William Sutton. Colour Sgt George Waller

Delhi, seat of the rebellion, had been recaptured by four columns in mid-September 1857 after nearly four months of siege war. British guns poured so much fire into the city's defences that shot ran short. Natives were paid half a rupee for every spent 18pdr roundshot recovered from mutineer fire. The muzzle-loading guns could fire almost anything. A handful of Englishmen besieged in a fortified house elsewhere fired door handles when their shot ran out.

Thirty Crosses were gained in retaking Delhi. The Royal Warrant provided for the award of the VC by election if a body of men had distinguished themselves equally. For each company one officer would be selected by officers present at the action, likewise one NCO by NCOs and two privates by fellow privates; four nominations in all. The method was first used officially during the Mutiny, for which eight ballots were held. In only two cases did the number of recipients correspond with the regulation four, though the War Office prudently raised no later objection. Each participating unit in the engagement received its 'ration' of Crosses for election, regardless of its contribution to the battle. Some commanders added further awards without authority while others reduced theirs to as little as one nomination.

VCs were awarded by election to five rather than four members of the 60th Rifles (King's Royal Rifle Corps) for their part in the recapture of Delhi. Lt Alfred Heathcote's gallantry was so consistent over the period that, instead of a date for his act of bravery, the citation gave its full duration 'June to September'. He repeatedly volunteered for services of extreme danger, once leading a fighting patrol with six men and killing eight or ten of the enemy, the Army's first forward move in that sector. On another occasion an advanced position was held by Heathcote and six men following his repeated refusal to obey orders to withdraw.

Pte James Thompson saved the life of his commanding officer on 9 July by dashing forward to aid Capt Wilton, who was surrounded by mutineers; Thompson killed two before further help reached them. Pte John Divane headed a successful charge of Indian troops on an enemy trench before Delhi, on 10 September. Three days later Bugler William 'Billie' Sutton volunteered to attempt a very dangerous but vital examination of a partial breach blown in the Kashmir Gate on the night before the final assault to recapture the city. Earlier he had rushed alone from the trenches and killed an enemy bugler in the act of sounding. The fifth man to be elected was Colour Sgt George Waller, who gained one of three VCs in the assault on Delhi's heavily defended Kabul Gate. He led a party through heavy fire on the 14th to take the enemy's guns, greatly assisting the capture of the gate.

Sir Colin Campbell's casual approach to the VC is related by Col Francis Maude in his *Memories of the Mutiny*. After the relief of Lucknow, at which Maude himself won the Cross, the 9th Lancers were required to nominate a trooper. As they had done no more than keep communications open and had not fought, they refused. When Campbell ordered them to produce a name, they chose to his fury a regimental bhisti or water carrier. The nomination did not go forward.

The Goughs – a Family Affair

Maj Charles Gough, Lt Hugh Gough (Indian Mutiny). Bt/Maj John Gough. Capt William Walker. Capt George Rolland (Somaliland, 1903)

There are only three known instances of the Victoria Cross being bestowed on father and son, and four where it went to brothers. Uniquely, the Gough family figures in both, and in having gained three Crosses. The first was awarded to Maj (later Gen) Charles J.S. Gough. His citation details four actions, the first on 15 August 1857, when he cut in to save the life of Lt Hugh Gough, his wounded brother, killing two of his assailants. The brothers served together in the Bengal European Light Cavalry and were rated among the most brilliant of the Indian Army's younger cavalry leaders. Three days later Charles led a troop in a charge, cutting down two sowars after desperate hand-to-hand combat with one of them. The following January at Shumsabad he ran the leader of the enemy's cavalry through with his sword. Unable to withdraw it, he killed two more with his revolver. The next month he dashed to assist a brother officer in trouble, killing his two assailants.

Lt (later Gen) Hugh Gough received his VC for two courageous actions, the first for leading his squadron in a charge across a swamp on 12 November 1857. Though vastly outnumbered, they captured two guns. His indigo-blue turban was sliced through with sword cuts and his horse wounded twice. He next distinguished himself near Jellalabad, Lucknow, showing a fine example to his regiment when ordered to charge the enemy's guns on 25 February 1858. In a series of single combats Hugh Gough had two horses killed under him that day. He was finally disabled by a musket ball through the leg when charging two sepoys with fixed bayonets. The rebel guns were taken.

Gen Sir Charles Gough's two sons followed him to become generals. The younger, Capt and Bt/Maj John Gough of the Rifle Brigade, earned the family's third Cross in Somaliland on 22 April 1903 while leading an exhausted column, short of ammunition and in retreat before a large force of Somalis. With Capts William Walker of the 4th Gurkha Rifles and George Rolland, 1st Bombay Grenadiers, and four native troops, he rode back through a hail of bullets to rescue a badly wounded Lt Bruce. They put him on a camel and fought their way back. Bruce died soon afterwards. Walker and Rolland also received VCs for their selfless act. Brig-Gen John Gough, 43, was killed in action in France in February 1915.

*   *   *

With comparative peace came abolition of the old East India Company. The Crown assumed direct rule of India in 1858, and a conditional amnesty was declared. The native army was reorganised to ensure it could never again mutiny. The balance of native to white troops was reduced to two to one. Artillery was placed exclusively in white hands. Widespread modernisation continued, and official interference in religion and social custom was avoided.

4

Growing Pains

*. . . under the Statutes we cannot recommend a dead
man, and a man cannot get the VC
unless he is recommended.*

*(Maj-Gen C. Grove, Military Secretary,
War Office, 15 May 1897)*

The Indian Mutiny raised unexpected issues affecting the
Victoria Cross. For better and for worse, the consequences
would shape the scope and procedures of the Cross for many
years before it reached maturity in the First World War. The
War Office remains responsible for administration of the award
on behalf of all the armed Services.

Posthumous VCs

*L/Cpl Alexander Thompson. Pte Edward Spence. QMS John
Simpson. Pte James Davis. Lt Walter Hamilton. Capt of the
Forecastle John Taylor RN. Sgt Alfred Atkinson. Lt Teignmouth
Melvill. Lt Nevill Coghill*

The Cross was not awarded posthumously until 1902, when
mounting anomalies and injustices finally broke the embargo.
The military and civil establishments had originally viewed the
award not as a decoration but as an order, like the Bath, to
which only the living can be appointed. Survivors of an act of
gallantry could thereby gain the VC and join an elite fraternity
of valorous brothers-in-arms. There could be no provision to
honour those who had fought just as valiantly beside them, and
died. The newly titled Secretary-for-War Lord Panmure firmly

held to this dogma. He proposed to name the Cross 'The Military Order of Victoria', and had its statutes drafted accordingly. When the draft reached the Palace for approval in December 1855, Prince Albert consulted the Queen before striking out all reference to an order, declaring it instead to be 'The Victoria Cross . . . a new Naval and Military Decoration'. The Queen wanted a medal, simple and supreme. The Victoria Cross was instituted on 29 January 1856, but Panmure defiantly ruled on 2 May that 'the VC is an *order* for the living' (emphasis in original). The Queen was not amused. Her secretary informed him in June 1857:

> The Queen thinks the persons decorated with the Victoria Cross might very properly be allowed to bear some distinctive mark after their name. The Warrant instituting the decoration does not style it an order, but merely a 'Naval and Military decoration', and a distinction; nor is it, properly speaking, an order, being not *constituted*. (Emphasis in original)

The Sovereign had demolished the basis of Panmure's edict at a stroke. He adroitly avoided all mention of the Cross in his reply. The VC Warrant had nothing to say either way concerning posthumous award, and Panmure's ruling led accordingly to a death-driven procedure. To become eligible for the Cross a fighting man had not only to survive his act of gallantry but also to stay alive to receive a recommendation, then evade death for months or even years until it was confirmed by the Queen. Should he die at any time before confirmation, the award was withheld. The *London Gazette* published the award and its citation following confirmation.

This procedure was shortened for the Indian Mutiny, where many, but not all, VCs were awarded under an alternative provision in the Warrant that enabled the GOC to confer the Cross on the spot, subject to confirmation by the Queen. It cut delay in exchanges with London, but there were unintended consequences. For the five officers and men who subsequently died after conferment and before confirmation, the Queen ruled that, as the VC had already been conferred, the decoration should be sent on to their widows or families 'with the expression of the satisfaction which it would have afforded HM to confirm the grant, had such Officer or Soldier survived'. The Queen must knowingly have opened this loophole in Panmure's ruling, through which posthumous VCs could now slip on the narrowest of grounds. It was all very well, but others were also dying before confirmation of award, whose families received no Cross because it had been recommended rather than conferred. Arcane distinctions such as these brought public incomprehension and bitterness.

The War Office ensured that authority for GOCs to confer the Cross under the 1856 Warrant was never exercised again; the posthumous loophole was closed. The War Office may also have welcomed this as a means of ending the discretionary powers of award held by distant and 'difficult' GOCs. Worldwide cable and radio communications made provisional conferment increasingly irrelevant. The Warrant of 1920 ended it.

Men died in the performance of supreme acts of valour that were not reported, because their officers knew the futility of doing so. Pte Patrick Cavanagh was a rare exception. He was the first to surmount a wall held by the enemy when it was stormed at Busserutgunge during the Mutiny. Maj-Gen Havelock's dispatch reported that Cavanagh was 'hacked to pieces while setting a brilliant example to his comrades . . . had he survived he should have won the VC which could never have glittered on a braver breast'.

Four men of the 42nd Regt The Black Watch gained VCs in a single day of the Mutiny, 15 April 1858. An attempt to blow the gate of rebel-held Fort Ruhya left casualties lying close beneath its walls on fire-swept ground. L/Cpl Alexander Thompson and Pte Edward Spence volunteered to assist Capt Café commanding

4th Punjab Rifles to retrieve the body of Lt Willoughby, to prevent its mutilation. Spence was severely wounded while giving covering fire from an exposed position. QMS John Simpson and Pte James Davis similarly braved heavy fire to bring in dead and wounded. The four performed identical deeds, but Spence died three days later. The other three lived to receive the Cross. Spence was gazetted with a memorandum stating that he would have been recommended for the VC had he survived. His family was left with a Press cutting for nearly fifty years before King Edward VII approved the award, and dispatch of the decoration to Spence's next of kin.

Eligibility for the VC became a macabre lottery, increasing in complexity as expedients and fudges were introduced by a War Office seeking to defend the indefensible. It was driven to falsifying its own paperwork for Lt Walter Hamilton of the Indian Army. He had died most valiantly in Afghanistan in 1879 before a recommendation for the Cross for an earlier act had reached the Palace. Panmure's procedure now automatically binned it. To avoid public outcry and ministerial humiliation, the War Office resorted to backdating its submission to the Queen to a discreet two days before Hamilton's death. The award went through.

Captain of the Forecastle John Taylor RN had rescued a badly injured soldier lying far beyond the forward trenches and under fire from Sebastopol's Redan. He was recommended for the Cross but came close to losing it at the last hurdle, the confirmation. Taylor died on the day of its gazetting, and the decoration duly went to his wife Elizabeth. She wrote to enquire if she might attend the Hyde Park presentation to receive her husband's Cross from the Queen's hands. The War Office coldly replied that it would be sent on by the Admiralty 'as part of his effects'.

Forty years later Gen Grove, Military Secretary at the War Office, was wrestling with the rule governing the forwarding of Crosses to relatives. In self-evident confusion he lamented to the Principal Under-Secretary on 15 May 1897:

I do not know on what grounds [the rule] was arrived at, or why in the case of a man who dies the day after the recommendation, the VC should be sent to his relatives, while in that of one who dies the day before the recommendation would have been made, it should not. At the same time, under the Statutes, we cannot recommend a dead man, and a man cannot get the VC unless he is recommended, so technically we cannot send to his relatives that which he could not get.

A mother's letter finally ended the absurdity, though not without a rearguard action from the High Command. Sgt Alfred Atkinson of the 1st Battalion The Yorkshire Regiment had distinguished himself in the Boer War at the battle of Paardeberg, 18 February 1900. He repeatedly left the safety of cover to cross open ground under heavy and close fire to fetch water for the wounded. On the seventh journey he was shot in the head, dying three days later before recommendation for award could be made. Mrs Atkinson wrote to the War Office in January 1902 enclosing a letter from her son's Adjutant attesting to his gallantry and explaining why the Victoria Cross had been denied him. She asked if the Office would use its influence to secure it.

The War Office recited the familiar mantra that award of a VC was unavailable to the dead. This hastily changed when Secretary of State for War Lord Brodrick declared in favour. The Army disagreed, fearing hordes of aggrieved service widows. A compromise proposed by Lord Roberts, the C-in-C, and approved by King Edward VII set 1899, the start of the Boer War, as a 'floor' prior to which no posthumous award would be considered. Six recently deceased, including Sgt Atkinson, were duly gazetted for VCs in August 1902, three of whom had already been gazetted with the memorandum formula stating that they would have been awarded VCs had they lived. That cleared Roberts's floor, but beneath it lay six more names of the dead from earlier years, all likewise gazetted by memorandum. They included Pte Edward Spence, who had been killed in the Mutiny (above), and Lts Teignmouth Melvill and Nevill Coghill, who had perished in the Isandhlwana disaster of 1879.

An irate Sir John Coghill wrote an 'intensely disagreeable and threatening letter' to Lord Brodrick. Coghill demanded VCs for his son and Melvill and ridiculed the artificial 'floor'. It collapsed under the weight of his argument, leaving a deeply embarrassed War Office frantically treading air. Lord Roberts threw Brodrick a lifeline, offering his support in seeking Royal approval to decorate the six, but no more. To their horror the Palace twice refused, relenting only in 1907 when King Edward was petitioned direct by Lt Melvill's widow. The *London Gazette* of 15 January announced posthumous Crosses for Melvill, Coghill, Spence and the other three. The final capitulation was timely. It brought no avalanche of retrospective applications. More than 180 posthumous VCs would be awarded in the coming First World War. The Warrant itself was not amended until 1920, at last declaring: 'It is ordained that the Cross may be awarded posthumously.'

Misconduct and Forfeiture

Midshipman Edward St John Daniel RN. Pte Edmund Fowler. Pte Valentine Bambrick. Piper George Findlater

The 1856 Warrant provided for the expulsion of a holder if 'convicted of Treason, Cowardice, Felony or of any infamous Crime, or if he be accused of any such offence and doth not after a reasonable time surrender himself to be tried for the same'. Liability to expulsion lasted for life, not just for the period of service, but the sovereign retained the right to restore the award. It was forfeited on eight occasions, the last in 1908.

Midshipman Edward St John Daniel, aged a mere 17, won his Cross while serving with the Naval Brigade in the Crimea. His fighting spirit came to notice on 5 November 1854 when he volunteered with others to fetch powder for the battery from an exposed ammunition wagon, its horses dead or disabled and under heavy fire. The 112lb zinc-lined wooden cases proved too much for him. After staggering back with the first, he made repeated journeys bringing ammunition and powder charges, to the cheers of the battery. At Inkerman he was aide-de-camp to the intrepid Capt William Peel VC, sticking close by as Peel led seven assaults. When the great Redan at Sebastopol was stormed on 18 June 1855, Peel was halfway up the fire-swept glacis when he fell, wounded in the arm. Daniel coolly applied a tourniquet before carrying the semi-conscious officer to cover. He was the only unwounded naval officer of the column, though his pistol case was cut open and his clothes torn by shot. These acts together secured him the VC.

Tragically, Daniel became drunken and dissolute and, in 1861, was the first man to forfeit the Cross. He was arrested on 21 June for sodomy with four subordinate officers. The Admiralty stated that he was 'accused of a disgraceful offence' and had deserted to evade inquiry. The alleged desertion appears to have been engineered by his Captain and the Admiral of the Mediterranean Fleet to avoid unwelcome revelations at a court martial. Edward Daniel fled to New Zealand, where as a lance corporal with the Armed Constabulary Field Force he died in 1868 during Fenian disturbances among the Irish goldminers.

Others were erased from the register of holders after convictions ranging from theft of ten bushels of oats to bigamy. Colour-Sgt Edmund Fowler of the Royal Irish Regiment faced forfeiture after conviction for embezzlement in 1887. He had won his VC as a private with the Cameronians in March 1879 after storming and clearing a cave sheltering armed Zulus who had just shot dead his officer. When the Secretary of State sought the Queen's permission to erase Fowler's name, however, her secretary replied that she could not bring herself to approve. Fowler had distinguished himself in earning the Cross and as his sole punishment was reduction to the ranks it appeared his offence could not have been serious. 'He is still considered fit to serve the Queen, and HM thinks he should retain his VC.' And so he did.

Those who forfeited the VC were also required to surrender the decoration itself. The Treasury Solicitor cautioned the War Office in 1908 that this was illegal, as the medal remained the property of the recipient. The War Office reacted with a catch-22 solution. It would not return forfeited Crosses unless recipients applied for them, but it would not so inform them. King George V ended the affair. His secretary wrote in 1920: 'The King feels so strongly that, no matter the crime . . . the decoration should not be forfeited. Even were a VC to be sentenced to be hanged for murder, he should be allowed to wear the VC on the scaffold.'

It all came much too late for Pte Valentine Bambrick of the 60th Rifles, born into a military family in India in 1837. His regiment was engaged in raising the siege of Delhi, and fought in the battle of Bareilly on 5–7 May 1858. Bambrick won his Cross there when he and Lt Ashburnham, his company commander, were cornered in a narrow street by three fanatical Muslim Ghazees. The two fought for their lives, the twice-wounded Bambrick cutting down one of the attackers. He later transferred to the 87th, taking his discharge from the Army at Aldershot in 1863. While celebrating his new freedom in a local pub, he intervened on discovering Commissariat Sgt Russell hitting a woman in an upstairs room, and gave him a thorough beating. Russell brought a charge of assault against Bambrick and accused him of stealing his medals. The woman, the only witness, disappeared. Russell and his cronies testified convincingly, and Bambrick was sentenced to three years in Pentonville. Already mortified by this injustice and the erasure of his name from the VC register, Bambrick was distraught on having to forfeit his Cross, unlawful though the measure was. He was found hanged in his cell three months after his jailing. A note expressed his despair at the loss of his award. Pte Valentine Bambrick was buried in an unmarked felon's grave. In 2002 the King's Royal

Rifle Corps Association dedicated a plaque to honour his memory and recognise the wrong that had been done to his name.

There were no more erasures after 1908. Though the eight forfeitures were never reinstated, their names have been restored to the list of holders. The present Warrant still provides for the cancellation and annulment of an award and removal of the recipient's name, but short of treason or terrorism it seems unlikely that this will ever again be exercised.

Exploitation of the VC for gain, while not misconduct, was considered discreditable and remains virtually unheard of. Piper George Findlater of the Gordon Highlanders won his VC for gallantry in the 1897 Tirah Campaign in India. Although shot in both feet during the charge on 20 October and in great pain, he sat erect under a heavy fire and continued playing 'Cock o' the North'. He was decorated by the Queen at Netley Hospital. His deed became renowned, and he was engaged to play the march on stage at London's Alhambra Theatre for £30 a week – far above his army pay. Some officers clubbed together to stop the performances, and Gen Sir Evelyn Wood, in full dress uniform, visited Dundas Slater, the manager, and offered to pay Findlater's salary if the act was cancelled. Slater laughingly refused, saying he had already spent £300 on promotion.

Award for Acts not in the Presence of the Enemy

Pte Andrew Walsh (no decoration). Pte Timothy O'Hea

Fire aboard a troopship caused the VC Warrant to be extended in August 1858 to include signal acts of valour *not* in the presence the enemy. The amendment was secured by the Army despite War Office objection. On 11 November 1857 the *Sarah Sands* was bound for India with a detachment of the 54th Foot and much powder and ammunition, when she caught fire 800 miles off Mauritius. In circumstances described as 'trying' in a special order of commendation read later to every regiment in the Army, volunteer soldiers formed human chains, and at huge risk most of the explosive was got overboard. Men choking in the burning and smoke-logged magazine escaped serious injury when conditions finally drove them out before the remaining powder exploded, blowing a hole in the stern. The flames, which also ignited the main yard and mast, were finally extinguished after eighteen hours. Many of the ship's crew had been at a distance, manning the boats laden with women and children. The wreck reached Mauritius twelve days later. The epic created great excitement at home. In July 1858 General Peel, Secretary-for-War, announced in the Commons that Her Majesty had approved an extension of the VC Warrant to include men aboard the *Sarah Sands*, and others in similarly desperate situations not in the presence of an enemy.

The War Office was highly displeased. There was talk that the VC had been cheapened. Sir Edward Lugard, Permanent Under-Secretary, informed the Army in February 1861 that the new Warrant could not be applied retrospectively. Any award to men aboard *Sarah Sands* would require a fresh Warrant specific to their acts, and anyway it was questionable, he ended, that anything should be done in view of the lapse of time. This was mendacious; the new Warrant made no distinction between past and future deeds, and Lugard's assertion flatly contradicted Peel's Commons statement. The Army returned to the issue in October 1863, but the War Office was adamant. Pte Andrew Walsh of the 54th, who had been singled out for recommendation, never received the VC.

Only six men were awarded the Cross under the 1858 Warrant. The gallantry of Pte Timothy O'Hea of the Rifle Brigade was so compelling that even the War Office could not prevent him gaining the first. During Canada's Fenian troubles an ammunition train was travelling from Quebec to Montreal on 9 June 1866. The locked boxcars were accompanied by a sergeant, O'Hea, and two other men of the Brigade. During a halt at Danville station one of the cars carrying 2,000lb of explosives was seen to be smoking and on fire. It was uncoupled and pulled clear at considerable risk. When the escort withdrew, O'Hea snatched the keys from his NCO and ran to the car, calling for a ladder and water. Pulling aside the cases, he found the seat of the fire and extinguished it single-handedly, averting a major explosion.

The Army's recommendation of the Cross for the 20-year-old Irishman from County Cork ran into a string of War Office objections. It considered that O'Hea was doing no more than his duty; the pension of £10 for life that accompanied the VC was in any case considered overgenerous for a private; a Board of Officers should have considered the matter; and, finally, since the 1858 Warrant had never been acted upon, it was deemed a dead letter. The Army won. A Board of Officers approved the recommendation with Peel's support, and O'Hea received his VC. He went to Australia in 1874 and joined an expedition searching for the remains of Leichhardt the explorer. Tim O'Hea died of thirst in the Queensland desert that November.

The War Office repeatedly tried to bury the 1858 Warrant, ensuring that it was never published in the *London Gazette*, and ignoring requests for copies. Only five more VCs were awarded under its little-known statutes, all of them for a somewhat marginally deserving surfing incident in the Andaman Islands in 1867. The War Office succeeded in killing off the Warrant in 1881, securing a new one stating unequivocally that the sole qualification for award of the VC shall be conspicuous bravery or devotion to the country 'in the presence of the enemy'. And so it remains. The limitation was occasionally ignored during the First World War when Crosses went to men who sacrificed their lives to save others, usually by throwing themselves across exploding munitions on practice ranges. Such deeds, including bomb disposal and extreme gallantry after capture, are now covered by the George Cross, which embraces civilians and members of the Armed Services for acts of supreme gallantry 'not on the field of battle'. The George Cross, 'the Civilian's VC,' was instituted by King George VI in September 1940. Its silver cross bearing an image of St George slaying the dragon and the words *For Gallantry* stands four square in honour beside the Victoria Cross.

Award of the VC to Civilians

The Revd James Adams. Master Archibald Bisset Smith, Mercantile Marine (T/Lt RNR)
Violette Reine Elizabeth Szabo GC. Noor Inayat Khan GC

Award of the Victoria Cross was refused point blank by a junior officer of the Indian Mercantile Marine in 1857. During the Persian War Freddie Warden undertook the hazardous task of landing a party of Sir James Outram's Indian troops from a transport to trace the movements of a large Persian force ashore. In the face of the greatest danger, the 21-year-old achieved his objective and brought back valuable information. On being told he had been recommended for the Cross, he declined, saying his achievement was not worthy of the honour. Frederick Warden had also distinguished himself during the Indian Mutiny. He became a sea captain before retiring to Bath, where he died in 1916.

After the Indian Mutiny the War Office put the narrowest possible interpretation on the December 1858 Warrant, which extended the Cross to civilians, ensuring that this became a dead letter. Twenty years later it sought to award the VC to a civilian. The circumstances are not to its credit. The Revd James Adams, Chaplain to the Kabul Field Force during the Second Afghan War of 1879, braved fire to free several trapped and near-drowning Lancers on 11 December after their horses had been hit and had fallen thrashing onto the men in a steep-sided and flooded ditch. The C-in-C India recommended him for a VC. Having sunk the Warrant the War Office was forced to raise another, but on such laughably narrow terms that only Adams ever qualified. The Warrant of 1881 confined civil award of the VC solely to members of Indian Ecclesiastical Establishments!

The continuing denial of the VC to civilians and especially to members of the Merchant Navy came to a head in 1917 following the heroism of Master Archibald Bisset Smith, a cargo ship's captain. He had engaged a heavily armed German raider with his single gun and inflicted considerable damage on the enemy before going down with his ship in the Atlantic on 10 March (see p. 119). The ever-practical Navy did not wait for amendment of the VC Warrant before awarding the Cross to this civilian hero. It posthumously conferred on him a Naval Reserve commission, backdated a judicious twelve days before his death. T/Lt Archibald Bisset Smith was awarded a Navy VC.

The pressing need completely to revise the VC Warrant had been frustrated in part by Queen Victoria's objection to tampering with what she regarded as Prince Albert's legacy. A new Warrant superseding all others was published in 1920. It extended the award to members of the Mercantile Marine while serving under naval or military authority, and to civilians of either sex serving under the orders of the forces. King George V was averse to the inclusion of women and civilians but was persuaded by the Army Council to approve their entitlement. It can fairly be said that this marked the maturity of the Victoria Cross, whose statutes have changed little since.

In practice, since its institution in 1940, the George Cross has superseded the VC for all civilians, including those who heroically faced the enemy on the battlefield or in captivity. No woman has received the VC, but four have been awarded the GC for gallantry in the Second World War. Three who served in enemy-occupied territory were eventually captured and resisted torture. Two of them, Violette Reine Elizabeth Szabo GC and Noor Inayat Khan GC, were shot.

VC 'Problem' Wars

Sudan, 1891 (Capt J.R. Beech). Basutoland, 1881 (Surgeon John McCrea). Vietnam, 1965 (WOII Kevin Wheatley)

Award of the VC to British, Colonial, and latterly Commonwealth forces has sometimes been disputed or refused on grounds that the act of gallantry was performed during hostilities to which the British government was not a party.

Capt J.R. Beech was refused a VC for his gallantry in the Sudan in 1891 because he happened to be on secondment to the 'wrong' army. When General Wolseley defeated the Egyptian army in 1882, the British government reckoned without the troublesome Sudan, which, as one of Egypt's responsibilities, now became that of its conquerors. Although the Egyptian army was quietly rebuilt under British command, Gladstone's government maintained the diplomatic fiction that Egypt remained a sovereign state under the Khedive. British officers who were 'lent' to the new army were ostensibly employees of the Khedive.

Beech was one such, seconded to command the Egyptian 20th Hussars. On 19 February 1891 a section of Sudan's fanatical army, which had killed General Gordon six years before, attacked the Egyptian garrison at Tokar. The Dervishes were repulsed by Beech's cavalry in an action in which he rescued an Egyptian officer attacked by three men. Beech, 60yd away, wheeled his horse and raced across, killing the first Dervish with a sabre blow to the head before being half pulled from his horse by the others. With his head in a neck-lock and seconds from death, he shortened his sword and drove it into the side of his assailant. The third Dervish was killed by arriving troopers. Beech had taken a sword cut in the arm but remained in the saddle all day. The Egyptian officer survived severe head injuries.

Beech was recommended for the VC by the GOC Egypt. The War Office refused, suggesting an Egyptian decoration. The Duke of Cambridge strongly disagreed, considering Beech's action 'one of the most deserving cases . . . that has ever been brought to [my] notice, and as this was an individual act on the part of a British officer . . . the gallantry was personal and independent of the operations directed under the Khedive's orders'. An undated note on the War Office file points out that, notwithstanding Beech's secondment to the Egyptian army, he remained a soldier of the Queen and an officer of the British Army 'and may be regarded as serving the Queen while so employed'. Nevertheless the Duke had to give way to preserve Egypt's sham independence. London gave the game away when the Military Secretary, Maj-Gen G.B. Harman, conveyed the decision to Cairo. Having explained that a VC could not be awarded 'for a service performed with the Egyptian Army in an operation in which no British troops were engaged', he added that Beech had been awarded a DSO.

Ten years earlier, Surgeon John F. McCrea of the Cape Mounted Yeomanry, South African Forces, was severely injured by a bullet in the chest during a fierce engagement with the Basutos at Tweefontein in South Africa on 14 January 1881. Having plugged the wound himself, he valiantly continued to recover and treat the wounded under fire for the rest of that day. The Colonial Office recommended award of the VC. The War Office responded that McCrea's act was performed by an officer of the Colonial Forces in hostilities of which the British government disapproved. The Colonial Office replied: 'The fact that the policy of the Cape Government which led to the hostilities during which the act of gallantry was performed was not approved by Her Majesty's Government should not prevent Surgeon McCrea's claim being considered on its merits.' McCrea received his Cross.

Despite the subsequent denial of the VC to Capt Beech, McCrea's VC had established an entitlement to the Cross regardless of political considerations. It appears to have been tested again during the Vietnam War. WO Kevin 'Dasher' Wheatley and WO R.J. Swanton of the Australian Army accompanied a search-and-destroy operation with Vietnamese irregulars in Tra Bong valley, Quang Ngai Province, on 13 November 1965. When they were ambushed in the open, the irregulars began to scatter and flee. Wheatley radioed for assistance and kept up fire. Swanton was shot in the chest and mortally wounded as he carried an injured man to cover.

A Vietnamese medic urged Wheatley to save himself, telling him Swanton was probably dead, but he refused to abandon his comrade. Having shot off his ammunition, Wheatley dragged Swanton into jungle. When the Viet Cong were only 10yd away, Wheatley refused to withdraw, and was last seen to pull the pins from two grenades before calmly awaiting the enemy, a grenade in each hand. Shortly afterwards two explosions were heard, followed by bursts of fire. The two bodies were found together next morning with multiple gunshots to the head. Kevin Wheatley could have escaped, but he set himself a higher and utterly selfless duty, which he knew meant his death.

Michael Crook records in his book *The Evolution of the Victoria Cross* that he was alerted by 'a well-informed source' to rumours that in 1963 the British government had declined to countenance award of British decorations to Australian servicemen in Vietnam because Britain was not involved in that conflict. The issue allegedly reached a critical point when the Australian authorities considered instituting their own gallantry medals including an Australian VC. If so, the implications must have persuaded the British government to withdraw its objections because VCs were awarded to Wheatley and later to three other members of the Australian Army in Vietnam. Wheatley's award was indeed delayed for thirteen months between recommendation and gazetting, leading to allegations of political stalling in London. However, Anthony Staunton, the respected Australian expert on VC matters, has researched official files in both countries and confirmed that the delay was completely the responsibility of the Australian authorities.

The Victoria Cross for Australia was established on 15 January 1991. Though identical, it replaces the Imperial Victoria Cross as part of an Australian system of honours and awards introduced in 1975. No VC Australia has yet been won.

5

Empire Wars, 1860–1913

'C' is for Colonies
Rightly we boast,
That of all the great nations
Great Britain has the most.

('An ABC for Baby Patriots', nursery rhyme, 1899)

Not a year of Victoria's long reign passed without the sound of gunfire somewhere in her dominions during brief and occasionally savage little actions in pursuit of trade, or its protection. More than a quarter of the world's population was controlled with an autocratic and sometimes harsh paternalism backed by the Army. Sea lanes were kept secure for the world's biggest merchant fleet by a Royal Navy maintained at the combined strengths of the next two largest navies. Adm Jackie Fisher, First Sea Lord in the early 1900s, declared Dover, Gibraltar, Cape Town, Singapore and Alexandria as the 'five strategic keys [that] lock up the world'. Britain held them all, a colossus of invention, manufacture, commerce and power. The slow decline of this great Empire followed the turn of the century and the Boer War.

Of the 1,351 VCs and 3 Bars won since the award's inception, better than every tenth Cross was gained in the forty years between the end of the Indian Mutiny in 1859 and the start of the Boer War. The 141 VCs honoured heroism and sacrifice in 31 'little' wars and rebellions from Crete to China, Africa to Afghanistan. The Boer War added 78, and 12 more followed before the First World War. Until the Boer War, the cost in British lives lost was taken for granted at home. It was the price of Empire.

THE THIRD CHINA WAR, 1859–1860

Lt Robert Rogers. Pte John McDougall. Lt Edmund Lenon. Lt Nathaniel Burslem. Pte Thomas Lane. Ensign John Chaplin. Hospital Apprentice Andrew Fitzgibbon. Lt-Col Gerald Graham. Drummer Thomas Flinn (Indian Mutiny). Pte John Moyse (no decoration)

The Third China War was one of the disreputable 'Opium Wars' instigated by Britain and abetted by France. The East India Company had a monopoly of the drug's production and distribution. China initially permitted its import in return for tea. The imperial government subsequently resisted the trade, receiving a taste of British gunboat diplomacy before treaties were signed that restored the drugs business and opened China's key ports to foreign trade. Britain became the major commercial and military power in the region. Signs of further Chinese intransigence in 1859 brought a punitive Anglo-French march on Peking. When their heavy guns reached the gates of the capital on 13 October the following year, the Chinese capitulated.

The Allied force of 18,000 troops had landed at the mouth of the Pei Ho river in July 1860. Their first obstacles were the formidable Taku Forts dominating the salt marshes. Artillery was brought up with great difficulty. The assault opened on 21 August with a bombardment of the North Fort by Armstrong's new breech-loading rifled 12pdrs – in action for the first time. A chance shot blew the Chinese magazine. It left their artillery without ammunition, but the walls were not breached. The attack switched to two English battalions, the 44th The Essex Regiment and the 67th Foot, The Hampshires, plus a French battalion. They met sustained small-arms fire as they waded to the foot of the walls. The storming parties competed to be the first with scaling ladders to mount the battlements under a ferocious fire, while engineers laid heavy charges against the walls. Lt Robert Rogers and Pte John McDougall, both of the 44th, and Lt Edmund Lenon, 67th, shared the same ladder. They were the first English troops to reach an embrasure and enter the fort. Rogers, first in, was severely wounded. All three received VCs for their magnificent courage and example.

Meanwhile Lt Nathaniel Burslem and Pte Thomas Lane, both of the 67th, were frantically pulling away partly dislodged stonework to enlarge a small breach made by the sappers. They were joined by Ensign John Chaplin bearing the Queen's Colours of the 67th, which he and Lane jammed into the torn masonry to rally support. They persevered despite fire from above until Burslem, followed by Lane, pushed through into the fort, where both were at once severely wounded. During fierce hand-to-hand fighting Chaplin was first to mount the fort's bastion, on which he planted the Colours. He was badly wounded in doing so. All three were awarded VCs. Thomas Lane was a hard-drinking Irish hell-raiser, an outstanding fighting man in battle or bar room. His Army career was studded with periods in cells. After his discharge in 1866 he fought in numerous colonial wars before deserting from the locally raised Landry's Light Horse in South Africa in 1881. This brought erasure of Lane's name from the register of VCs. He also forfeited his medal, though the Warrant made no provision for this, and the accompanying pension ceased. He resumed his dubious African adventures, dying in Kimberley in 1889.

The most surprising of the seven Crosses gained that day went to Hospital Apprentice Andrew Fitzgibbon of the East India Company, aged 15 years and 3 months. He was attached to the 67th, and that morning accompanied them to a position less than 500yd from the Fort. Ordered to dress the wounds of a stretcher-bearer, he left cover to do so and came under very heavy fire. On completion he ran across the bullet-swept ground to another injured man and was himself severely wounded. He shares the honour of being the youngest holder of the VC with Drummer Thomas Flinn (North Staffs Regt; Prince of Wales's), who charged rebel guns during the Indian Mutiny and fought two gunners hand to hand despite his wounds.

The indomitable Lt-Col Gerald Graham VC was also present. As already recounted, he received his Cross for leading a ladder party at the assault of Sebastopol's Redan in 1855. While under fire from the North Fort, the burly 6ft 4in engineer was directing construction of a pontoon bridge over a canal. He rode up to a fellow officer who, as he straightened to speak, laid a hand on Graham's leg to get his balance. In an easy conversational tone Graham remarked: 'Don't put your hand there old chap for I have just had a bullet through my thigh.'

Loyalty and extreme defiance of the enemy had earlier brought the execution of Pte John Moyse of the Buffs after he and his sergeant were captured by Tartar cavalry on 13 August. They were taken before mandarin Tsan-koo-lin-sin and ordered to kow-tow – touch foreheads to the ground. When Moyse refused, he was told he would be beheaded unless he obeyed. Declaring he wore the Queen's uniform and would sooner die than disgrace his country, he was instantly executed. The sergeant very understandably complied, and was released under flag of truce. In preferring a horrific death to submission, John Moyse deserved the highest military honour from the nation for which he so valiantly chose to die. Capture and death debarred it.

AFGHANISTAN, 1877–1880

Lt Walter Hamilton. Gunner James Collis

Between 1863 and 1901 Britain fought twenty wars in Afghanistan, the harsh and mountainous buffer zone separating India from Russia, to maintain supremacy on this frontier and to deter Russian ambitions. The fighting spirit, endurance and resourcefulness of the Pathan warriors and the indomitable qualities of their invaders earned mutual respect, giving the many campaigns an exaggerated romance at home. Russia sent a Mission to Afghanistan in 1877, which was welcomed by the Amir. It brought a curt British ultimatum. Either the Amir accepted a resident British envoy in Kabul or the issue would be resolved by force. When he refused, the British invaded Afghanistan with 25,000 troops whose successes forced Kabul to sue for peace in May 1879. The Mission was established.

Lt Walter Hamilton of the Indian Army's famous Corps of Guides had found himself the only surviving officer of his regiment during a cavalry charge at Futtehabad on 2 April that year. He spurred forward, cheering on his men. Dowlat Ram in the Guides' distinctive indigo blue turban and khaki uniform rode beside him until the Sowar's horse fell dead, entangling his leg in bridle and stirrup leather as it crashed. Hamilton pulled hard round, jumped his charger into a dense knot of sword-wielding Afghans about to butcher the trapped Guide, and emerged unscathed after cutting down three. Dowlat Ram caught a riderless horse, and the two resumed the charge to a victorious conclusion. Hamilton was recommended for the VC, but the Duke of Cambridge, C-in-C of the British Army in London, considered he had done no more than his duty and refused to submit it to the Queen. When representations from the India Office eventually won Cambridge round, 23-year-old Hamilton was dead.

He had commanded the defence force of seventy Guides at the new Kabul embassy when the compound was stormed by a huge mob on 3 September. It overwhelmed them before firing the Residency and murdering the Ambassador and his entire staff. One or two Guides survived, reporting that Hamilton was last seen leading a handful of his men in a suicidal charge into the thick of the mob, cutting their way through in a last act of supreme defiance before they were hacked to pieces. With sword in one hand and pistol in the other, Hamilton took five rebels with him before he was engulfed. As already recounted, his death rendered him ineligible for the Cross, despite the earlier recommendation and this second suicidally courageous act. Fear of public outrage caused the War Office to bend its already discredited rules. The submission to the Queen was backdated to two days before Hamilton's death. The VC decoration accordingly went to his family.

Gen Roberts VC entered Kabul in October 1879 and hanged the ringleaders, before leading a punitive and costly expedition. The Maiwand disaster on 27 July 1880 became a fight to save the guns in a rout. James Collis of 'E' Battery, 'B' Brigade, was a 24-year-old limber gunner in the retreat to Kandahar. Around noon that day, in ferocious heat, well-armed Afghan tribesmen had charged in among them, the gunners fighting back with handspikes and whatever else came to hand. The survivors were pursued by cavalry, a brave rearguard of the 66th dying almost to a man. The gun teams pulling limbers laden with wounded were furiously whipped up beneath a lengthening pall of red dust. Hearing nothing above the thunder of wheels and hooves, Collis was grazed above the eye as a sabre flashed before his face. While his bearded pursuer wheeled for another cut, Collis reached for a carbine and shot him off his horse. The pace slackened as the enemy fell back. Collis and his crew pushed on alone throughout the night and next day, halting only late in the afternoon. He procured the first water for the wounded since the fight had begun. On his second trip he saw a dozen Afghan cavalrymen approaching. As the exhausted horses were spurred to get gun and wounded away, he remained with a rifle to buy them time, killing two cavalrymen and a horse. The Afghans halted, returning fire in the apparent belief that they faced a rearguard. As they again advanced on Collis, Gen Nuttall arrived with native cavalry and saw them off; he then took the young man's name.

The gunner continued to display exceptional courage. He received the Cross on General Roberts's recommendation, but things went badly wrong in later years. After discharge in 1881 he served eighteen months hard labour for bigamy. Though Collis was no longer a soldier and his crime was a civil offence, his name was removed from the VC register and he lost the pension. The decoration itself was forfeited, the police having to redeem it for 8s (40p) from a pawnbroker. By 1913 Collis was in a Cambridge workhouse before re-enlisting aged 58 on the outbreak of the First World War. He was discharged unfit from the Suffolk Regt in 1917 and died the following year, receiving a full military funeral. His sister petitioned the King for restoration of her brother's award. George V assured her that his name would be inscribed with those of the other VCs on the Royal Artillery Memorial. The King was reluctantly obliged however to take Winston Churchill's advice as War Minister, and refuse the petition. Collis was the seventh of eight VCs to be struck off the Register before the practice was dropped after 1908 at the request of King Edward VII. There would be no official reinstatement for any of them in their lifetime, but they are now listed as holders.

ZULULAND

Isandhlwana, 22 January 1879

Lt Teignmouth Melvill. Lt Nevill Coghill. Pte Samuel Wassall

Briton, Boer and Bantu were at permanent loggerheads in the vast plains of South Africa. The British had occupied the Cape in 1806 to create a staging post for their East India possessions. The Dutch settlers who were already there, Boer or Afrikaner, resented Britain's even-handed administration of the Cape Colony's white and black subjects. British abolition of slavery in 1833 drove many Boers to trek north to establish their own republics. In the Cape Colony, irksome frontier wars hardened British attitudes to hostile tribes. Discovery of diamonds in the 1860s changed everything. The colony became a valuable asset requiring a passive black workforce and regional stability. The British government proposed a South African federation with the Transvaal and Orange Free State territories of the Boers. Sir Bartle Frere the new Governor of the Cape Colony determined first to emasculate the neighbouring – and presently peaceable – Zulu kingdom of chief Cetewayo, whose superbly disciplined army of 40,000 warriors posed a future threat. Frere misled London into believing Cetewayo planned war. The Colonial Secretary wrote to him: 'we entirely deprecate the idea of entering on a Zulu war to settle the Zulu question'. Frere and the colonists nevertheless provoked Cetewayo into a battle. In the space of a single day it produced one of the worst military disasters of Britain's colonial history, and one of its most notable feats of arms.

The colony assembled an army of 5,000 European infantry, 1,200 mounted Europeans and 8,000–9,000 native levies. Lord Chelmsford its commander, who had been at the fall of Sebastopol with the Grenadier Guards, weakened his invading force by breaking it into three dispersed columns for the 60-mile drive on Ulundi, Cetewayo's capital. He led the centre column, crossing the Buffalo river at Rorke's Drift on 11 January 1879. On the 19th they reached Isandhlwana, a flat-topped hill with steep-sided flanks on all sides overlooking an open plain. Chelmsford set camp on its crown before moving on with the main body before dawn on the 22nd in search of Cetewayo's army. He left an inadequate rearguard of six companies of the 24th The South Wales Borderers with two guns, some mounted volunteers and native troops. They were joined later that morning by Col Durnford RE from Rorke's Drift, bringing a rocket battery and 300 native levies.

As senior officer, Durnford assumed command from Bt/Lt-Col Pulleine, who had unaccountably ignored Chelmsford's orders to draw in the thin defences to mass their firepower. Instead he had dispersed them before detaching part of the already slender force and departing on a probing mission towards the enemy. His column returned in disarray, pursued by 20,000 plumed and chanting Zulus. Cetewayo's army engulfed Durnford's force and the camp's forward positions, taking huge casualties literally in its stride before sweeping across the 300yd-wide campsite, butchering all who stood their ground. Of the 950 Europeans and 850 Natal levies, only some 55 and 350 respectively got away. There were no wounded, no missing. The Zulus spared none, including their own severely wounded.

Isandhlwana produced three VCs. When all was lost, Lt Teignmouth Melvill, Adjutant of the 1st Battalion, retrieved the precious Colours and rode off with them hell for leather. As the Zulus held the road to Rorke's Drift, he and other fugitives made for the Buffalo river across 6 miles of precipitous hills. They were pursued by warriors agile as cats and almost as fast as the fleeing horses picking their way over the high ledges. Melvill, Lt Nevill Coghill also of the 24th, and Lt Higginson of the Natal Native Regiment reached the swollen and fast-flowing Buffalo more or less together. When Coghill made the far bank, he turned to see the other two had been swept off their mounts and carried to a large rock in midstream, where they clung, Melvill still encumbered with the heavy black leather tube. Coghill could have ridden clear, but instead rode back into the river to help. The bank they had left was filling with armed Zulus who blazed away, killing Coghill's horse. He swam to the rock, where Melvill let go of the Colours as all three struggled for their lives to reach the far bank. Higginson landed further down and got away to tell the story. Melvill and Coghill were last seen attempting to escape before sitting, probably wounded, and too exhausted to go further. Their bodies were found close to those of several Zulus, killed by them in a last desperate stand.

The third VC went to Pte Samuel Wassall of the 80th The South Staffordshire Regiment. He too reached the river bank. Finding Pte Westwood of his regiment drowning, Wassall dismounted at imminent risk to his own life as his pursuers came in view. He swam out to bring Westwood back before remounting under a hail of bullets and dragging his barely conscious comrade across the river. Both men got away.

The Colours of the 24th were later recovered, to be decorated by the Queen with a wreath in a simple ceremony at Osborne the following year. By her command the pole was inscribed with the names of Lts Melvill and Coghill. Gen Sir Garnet Wolseley, who had not been present at the battle, argued that they should have died with their men on the hilltop. He overlooked the fact that regimental Colours were as sacrosanct as guns, and it was an officer's duty to preserve either from capture at any cost. Melvill and Coghill were gazetted to the effect that they would have been awarded the VC had they lived. Their families were left with an abiding sense of injustice for twenty-seven years until Melvill's widow successfully petitioned King Edward VII in 1907. Crosses for both officers were awarded posthumously.

Rorke's Drift, 22–23 January 1879

Lt John Chard. Lt Gonville Bromhead. Surgeon Maj James Reynolds. Pte Frederick Hitch. Cpl William Allan. Pte John Williams (b. Fielding). Pte Henry Hook. Pte Robert Jones. Pte William Jones. Cpl Ferdnand Schiess. Acting Assistant Commissary James Dalton

The mission station at Rorke's Drift lay on the Natal side of the Buffalo river crossing into Zululand. Its two thatched buildings comprised Chelmsford's main supply depot and hospital. On 22 January, the day of the Isandhlwana disaster, Col Durnford's morning departure with a detachment left Lt John Chard RE in command of the post. His depleted garrison comprised Lt Gonville Bromhead's eighty-four men of B Company, the 2nd/24th South Wales Borderers, and a company of the Natal Native Contingent. Surgeon Maj James Reynolds tended thirty-six invalids in the hospital. Chard, aged 32, and Bromhead, 33, were experienced officers, though neither was highly esteemed by his superiors. Chard was thought slow while Bromhead suffered hearing problems.

From the tide that had just swept away six companies of the 24th at Isandhlwana, an eddy of over 3,000 triumphant warriors now surged on to engulf Rorke's Drift. Word of the disaster and of their imminent danger reached the post at about 15.30 with the arrival of remnants of Durnford's irregular cavalry. It was too late to make a run for it – the post had no defences and there was perhaps an hour to improvise. The store was emptied. Sacks of flour, furniture and upturned wagons barricaded an area between the hospital at one extremity and the store at the other. A run of yard wall completed the perimeter. When the Zulu advance guard was sighted at 16.20, most of the post's native troops slipped away, their officer and a European sergeant joining them. Parting shots from disgusted defenders killed the sergeant. Missionary Otto Witt also made off, later billing the Army for repairs to his station. Chard's defenders were down to 104 of all ranks fit enough to face South Africa's most formidable native army. With so few, a smaller rearguard position was prepared by dividing the compound into two halves with a separating barricade. What followed is best described through the deeds of some of those who were honoured with the Cross.

As the Zulus neared, Bromhead sent Pte Frederick Hitch to the roof to observe. Hitch recalled that they were massing behind a rise. 'How many?' called Bromhead. 'Four to six thousand', shouted Hitch. The reply came back 'Is that all? We can manage that lot very well.' The attack came in the tribe's traditional 'Buffalo' form, with two flanking horns, the central thrust as the chest, and behind it a powerful reserve, the loins. Hitch joined defenders at a gap, bayoneting warriors as each leapt through into the yard until the break was piled with Zulu dead. Hitch noted their indifference to bullets and fear of bayonets. Wave followed wave, the defenders grouping and regrouping to plug gaps and meet changing pressure points. The Revd George Smith constantly circled the perimeter, passing ammunition with words of quiet encouragement. Hitch and Cpl William Allan greatly assisted communication between the fire-swept store and hospital. Both received serious wounds but after attention they insisted on becoming ammunition carriers and so continued to the end.

Ptes John Williams and Henry Hook helped defend the hospital. Between massive onslaughts, warriors carrying muskets and Martini rifles kept up a furious but ill-directed fire on the compound, resulting in a third of the defenders' total casualties. Hook picked off five Zulu riflemen in succession as they left cover to fire. Bromhead bravely led several successful counter-attacks to drive off warriors massing around the hospital. It became necessary to reduce the perimeter at about 18.00 and withdraw to the smaller compound around the store. Those in the hospital could escape only after holes had been cut in the internal party walls to reach a room whose window overlooked the compound. As Williams, Hook and Ptes Robert and William Jones worked frantically to hack out a passage, Zulus fired the thatched roof above them. Warriors burst into the far room, spearing two patients and turning on Ptes Joseph Williams and Horrigan, who fought back, killing several before they were overwhelmed on the wrong side of the first hole. The defenders dragged patients from room to smoke-filled room, bayoneting warriors as their stabbing assegais emerged from the holes behind them. With all but two of the remaining patients, they made it through the small window and across to the store compound under covering fire.

The rushes continued into the night, the physically imposing Zulus fighting as bravely as the little garrison. Providentially for the defenders, the burning hospital lit their perimeter. Surgeon James Reynolds brought up ammunition whenever he had to cross the open ground. Cpl Ferdnand Schiess of the Natal Native Contingent, a Swiss from Berne, had hobbled from the hospital on a wounded foot to join the defence, fighting like a tiger. Incensed to see Storekeeper Alexander Byrne killed by a sniper concealed in the abandoned compound, Schiess limped along the defence line, shot the rifleman and killed two others. Rifles became so hot that jams were frequent. The weapons were repeatedly wielded as clubs when there was no time to reload. Wave after wave broke on the barricades until pressure eased at around 22.00. Rifle fire and spear throwing continued into the small hours. By 04.00 the warriors were retiring. The exhausted survivors still had to pull down the gutted hospital walls and collect weapons around the body-strewn perimeter, denying cover and arms to any returning host.

The deeply shocked remnants of Chelmsford's approaching main force passed silently by the retreating Zulus, neither group having the stomach for more fighting. Expecting to find a mini-Isandhlwana, the troops were met with cheering survivors ringed by well over 400 Zulu dead. The defenders had suffered seventeen killed and twelve wounded. The garrison secured eleven Victoria Crosses, the most ever for a single action. It was impressive testimony of its leadership that losses were so few, but recriminations followed. Chelmsford was diligently blaming others for Isandhlwana. The triumph at Rorke's Drift was vulnerable to some compensating inflation in the distribution of awards. Chelmsford recommended Bromhead for a VC without consulting his regimental commander, and Chard as senior officer for another, though Chard was never consulted on the distribution of awards to others of the garrison. Gen Wolseley later remarked: 'I presented Major Chard RE with his Victoria Cross; a more uninteresting or more stupid fellow I never saw. [Col Sir Evelyn] Wood tells me he is a most useless officer, fit for nothing. I hear in the camp that the man who worked hardest at Rorke's Drift was the Commissariat Officer [James Dalton] who has not been rewarded at all.' Acting Assistant Commissary Dalton, a locally engaged ex-Sergeant Major, waited many months before he too received the Cross. Bromhead, who had distinguished himself, recommended VCs for six members of his company, Cpl William Allan and Ptes Frederick Hitch, Henry Hook, William and Robert Jones, and John Williams. VCs also went to Cpl Schiess and Surgeon James Reynolds.

The disaster of Isandhlwana faded. Lts Chard and Bromhead were promoted brevet majors, Chard becoming the first RE officer to skip a captaincy. The Queen commanded that their names be added to those of Melvill and Coghill on the colour pole of the 24th. With customary understatement their citations for the VC described the circumstances as 'trying'. Frederick Hitch became a commissionaire at the Royal United Services Institute. A thief snatched the Cross off his chest one day, never to be recovered. King Edward VII ordered a replacement, which Lord Roberts duly presented to him. That too had disappeared at Hitch's death in 1913. In later life he was a 'cabbie'. His funeral in Chiswick was attended by the Colonel and many others of his old regiment, and by 1,500 fellow taxi-drivers with whom he was on strike when he died. The Fred Hitch award for gallantry by cabbies continues in being. Henry Hook bought his discharge in 1880, later working at the British Museum. The crippled Ferdnand Schiess was the first man serving with South African Forces under British command to receive the VC. Nearly six years later, when his health was broken after he had lived in poverty since his discharge, RN sailors clubbed together to pay his passage home. Schiess never made it, dying at sea off Angola. Robert Jones suffered badly from recurring dreams of that night. After service with the 24th in India, he became a farm labourer in Wiltshire, raising a large family. In 1898 he was found dead beside a shotgun.

Lord Chelmsford defeated the Zulus at Ulundi in July 1879 before his recall to London. As a close friend of the Queen he was never held to account for the disaster. Prime Minister Disraeli refused to receive him officially.

THE ANGLO-BOER WAR, 1899–1902

Unfinished business in South Africa drove Britain into a hugely expensive conflict with a much more formidable opponent in 1899. Having subjugated the tribes in Cape Colony and Natal, she pursued the goal of a British-dominated federation with the Boer republics. There the stolid Calvinist Dutch-speaking settlers of the Transvaal and the Orange Free State prepared to fight colonial interference to the death. Tense exchanges between Britain and the Boers ended on 11 October 1899 with a declaration of war from Paul Kruger, President of the Transvaal, and President Steyn of the Orange Free State. The entire Boer population numbered little more than 100,000, but its farmer 'commandos' were fine horsemen, crack shots, and knew how to use and fight from cover. The combination of mobility, firepower and fieldcraft proved deadly against the traditional close-order battle formations of brilliantly uniformed soldiers of the Empire. It demanded a radical and more intellectual British generalship. Early failures forced a complete change in the command of the army in the field before the war was won, but the great generals were all Boers.

Exhaustion on both sides brought a peace treaty in May 1902, which gave Britain the political supremacy she sought. The Boers received cash aid to rebuild and restock their farms, the promise of self-government for the republics, and assurances of their continuing dominion over the native population. The war had cost Britain over £200 million, the mobilisation of nearly 300,000 men, and 52,000 dead or wounded. The rest of the world took note of the nation's unshakeable will to maintain its imperial power against all comers and at any price, but in truth this war heralded the slow decline of the British Empire over the next 100 years. The winning of it earned seventy-eight Victoria Crosses.

Colenso, 15 December 1899

Cpl George Nurse. Capt Walter Congreve. Capt Harry Schofield. Lt The Hon. Frederick H.S. Roberts. Pte George Ravenhill. Capt Hamilton Reed. Maj William Babtie

The Boers invaded Natal and Cape Colony. Kruger sought to entrap the British and paralyse the railways on which they relied for supply. After initial successes, local British forces were driven back to become besieged in Mafeking, Kimberley and Ladysmith. The brave, popular but intellectually limited General

Sir Redvers Buller VC was appointed C-in-C and dispatched from London with an army of 47,000 men. He formed three columns to break the sieges, personally leading a drive on Ladysmith with 20,000 troops. It ended in rout at Colenso on the Tugela river on 15 December 1899. The serving of the guns at Colenso and later attempts to recover them are among the most heroic actions of the Royal Field Artillery.

In support of the attack earlier that day the dashing but reckless Col Charles Long had brought up two 6-gun batteries and a shore party with six naval guns under Lt F.C.A. Ogilvy of the *Terrible*. The exact whereabouts of concealed Boer guns and entrenchments just beyond the Tugela was unknown. Long's orders were to position his batteries well back from the river, out of rifle shot. The stipulation made it a job for the longer barrels and range of Ogilvy's 12pdrs. Dismissing Ogilvy's protests, however, Long outdistanced his infantry cover and the ox-drawn naval limbers and, disregarding Gen Buller's instructions, positioned the batteries less than 1,000yd from the river. As they unlimbered and the teams were being taken back, Gen Louis Botha unleashed so intense and continuous a fire of Mauser and shrapnel from unseen positions overlooking them that the situation rapidly became untenable. Men and horses fell in ragged heaps, but the 15pdrs maintained fire, gunners covering for the fallen as crews thinned. Long was gravely wounded. Only when they had emptied the first line of ammunition wagons and casualties reached a third of their number did his acting commander order withdrawal to a donga or rocky hollow 50yd to the rear. Four men stood fast, continuing to serve their gun until all were dead. It was impossible to move the guns back. Horses were felled before they and the limbers reached the batteries. Ogilvy's guns lay further back, less cut up and still firing.

Observing the line of abandoned guns, Buller and his staff rode to a large depression 500yd behind it, which sheltered most of the unwounded crews and horse teams. Buller had

1. *Right*. The first investiture of the VC. Queen Victoria decorates Sgt-Maj John Grieve, one of 62 recipients that day. To general surprise she remained mounted. Hyde Park, 26 June 1857.

2. *Below*. The two captured Chinese cannon from whose cascabels nearly every VC has been cast since December 1914. Today's Crosses originate from the left-hand gun, identifiable as having a less heavily hooped barrel.

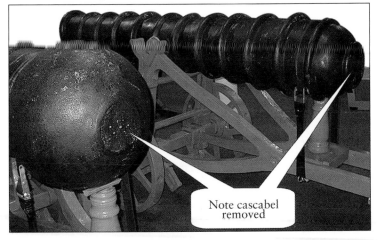

Note cascabel removed

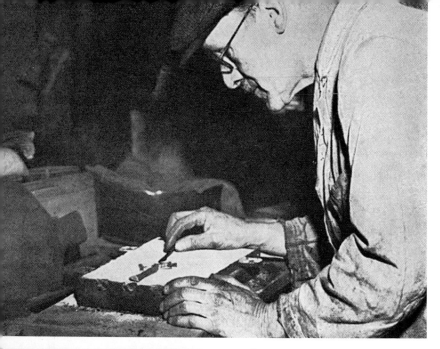

3. *Above.* Specialist VC caster Mr Alec Forbes prepares a sand mould at the foundry of Messrs R. Owen Ltd, Clerkenwell, EC1. 1945.

4. *Left.* Alec Forbes melts gunmetal before casting his 751st VC. 1945.

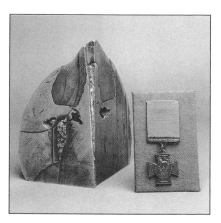

5. *Right.* Today's ingot of VC metal. The 358oz block is good for some 90 more Crosses.

6. *Above.* A/Mate Charles Lucas, the first VC, disregarded warning shouts and picked up a live Russian shell, heaving it overboard just before it exploded. Crimean War, 21 June 1854. (after a drawing by E.T. Dolby).

7. *Right.* Charles Lucas ended his naval career as a rear admiral.

8. *Left.* Sgt Luke O'Connor, though badly wounded, snatched the precious Colour from dying Lt Anstruther during the Battle of the Alma. He gallantly carried it throughout that day. Crimea, 20 September 1854.

9. *Left*. Troop Sgt-Maj John Berryman had his horse shot beneath him at Balaclava. Under severe Russian fire, he attended an injured officer before carrying him to safety. Crimea, 25 October 1854.

10. *Right*. Lt William Hewett RN (Naval Bde) refused orders to spike his gun and withdraw. He and his crew fought on, beating back the Russians. Crimea, 26 October 1854.

11. *Left*. Lt Henry Havelock was sent to order a regiment to take a rebel gun delaying the advance on Cawnpore. Seeing no officer, he rallied the troops and rode steadily ahead through heavy fire. The gun was captured. Indian Mutiny, 16 July 1857.

12. *Right*. AB William Hall RN (Naval Bde), the first black man to win the VC. He and a wounded officer were sole survivors of two gun's crews attacking rebel defences. Lucknow, 16 November 1857.

13. Thomas Kavanagh, a civilian, crossed rebel lines in a daring mission to guide in the first column sent to relieve Lucknow. Indian Mutiny, 9 November 1857.

14. Pte Thomas Lane was among the first to break into one of the heavily defended Taku Forts in the Third China War. 21 August 1860.

15. Gnr James Collis, his limber laden with wounded in a desperate retreat, stayed behind to hold off 12 Afghan pursuers. The gun team got away. Afghanistan, 27 July 1880.

16. 'Last Stand of the 24th Regt of Foot, Isandhlwana.' Charles Edwin Fripp (1854–1906). Isandhlwana saw one of the worst military disasters in Britain's colonial history. Some 950 European and 850 native troops were overrun by 20,000 Zulus. South Africa, 22 January 1879.

17 & 18. Pursued by Zulus, Lt Teignmouth Melvill (*left*) rode off with the precious Colours of the 24th when all was lost at Isandhlwana. Lt Nevill Coghill (*right*) attempted to save Melvill's life. Both perished.

19 & 20. The defenders at Rorke's Drift during the Zulu War gained 11 VCs, the most ever for a single action. Acting Ass't Commissary James Dalton (*left*) and Pte Frederick Hitch (*right*) were among them. Natal, S. Africa, 22/23 January 1879.

21. *Right*. Cpl George Nurse endured a firestorm in successfully recovering one of the guns abandoned with heavy loss of life at Colenso. Boer War, 15 December 1899.

22. *Left*. Pte Robert Scott. He and Pte James Pitts fought alone for 15 hours, becoming the only survivors of Caesar's Camp, Ladysmith. South Africa, 6 January 1900.

23 & 24. Under heavy fire, Lt John Grant (*left*) led a storming party on hands and knees up a near-precipitous rock-face to take Tibet's Gyantse Jong fortress (*below*). 6 July 1904.

25 & 26. Lt Maurice Dease (*below left*) died of wounds while commanding two machine guns defending a canal bridge near Mons. His was the first VC of the First World War. Pte Sidney Godley (*right*) then held the bridge alone and under fire for two hours. Belgium, 23 August 1914.

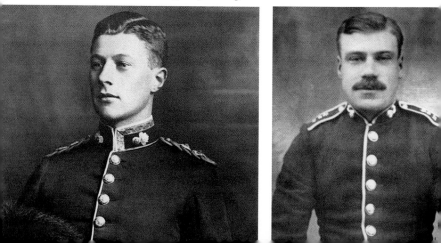

27 & 28. The valiant stand of Capt Edward Bradbury's 'L' Battery at Nery, France, 1 September 1914 (*above*). Capt Bradbury (*right*) died serving the last gun, beside which two more Crosses were won that day.

29. *Above*. 2/Lt William Rhodes-Moorhouse RFC bombed a rail junction in arduous circumstances. He died of wounds the next day. Courtrai, Belgium, 26 April 1915.

30. *Right*. The first of only three double-VCs honoured Lt Arthur Martin-Leake RAMC, for repeatedly recovering wounded under fire in two wars. Boer War, 8 February 1902. Bar, Zonnebeke, Belgium, 29 October–8 November 1914.

31. *Left*. Cdr Edward Unwin RN commanded a transport at V Beach, Gallipoli. Under intense fire he secured a bridge of lighters and recovered many wounded. 25 April 1915.

32. *Below*. Pte William McFadzean threw himself across a spilled box of grenades, knowing several would explode in seconds. His sacrifice saved many. The Somme, 1 July 1916.

33 & 34. T/Lt-Col Roland Bradford (*below, left*), and his brother Lt-Cdr George Bradford RN (*right*). Roland Bradford's inspired leadership and gallantry earned his VC on the Somme, 1 Oct 1916. George Bradford died after securing a vital troop transport under terrific fire during the Zeebrugge Raid, Belgium, 22/23 April 1918.

35. Cdr Gordon Campbell RN commanded a heavily armed 'mystery ship', which was torpedoed off Ireland. As his vessel settled, he coolly lured the U-boat to the surface, destroying it. Irish Sea, 17 February 1917.

36. *Above*. 2/Lt Alan McLeod RFC and his observer downed three triplanes. Their FK8 on fire, McLeod climbed out on to the lower wing and controlled the machine to a crash-landing. Albert, France, 27 March 1918.

37. *Right*. The second double-VC. Surgeon Capt Noel Chavasse, RAMC, repeatedly ignored his own wounds while tending injured in the field. He died after a direct hit on his aid post. Guillemont, 9 August 1916. Bar, Wieltje, 31 July–2 August 1917.

38. The first VC of the Second World War. Lt-Cdr Gerard Roope RN, commanding a lone destroyer, engaged the heavy cruiser *Admiral Hipper*. He finally rammed and holed it before going down with his ship. Norwegian Sea, 8 April 1940.

39. 2/Lt Richard Annand led three critical counter-attacks, gaining the Army's first VC of the war. River Dyle, Belgium, 15/16 May 1940. Pictured with his wife Shirley at the Palace.

40. Flt Lt James Brindley Nicolson's Hurricane was hit by a Messerschmitt over Southampton. Wounded and on fire, he downed his attacker before baling out. His was the only Fighter Command VC of the war. 16 August 1940.

41. Cpl John Edmondson, Australian Forces, fought hand-to-hand at Tobruk. Mortally wounded, he saved the life of his officer. North Africa, 13/14 April 1941.

42. Left. The third and last VC and Bar was bestowed on Capt Charles Upham, New Zealand Forces. An outstanding leader, he excelled in close-quarter fighting. Crete, 22/30 May 1941. Bar, Western Desert, 14/15 July 1942.

43, 44, 45. HM submarine *Thrasher* after removal of two unexploded 100lb bombs by Lt Peter Roberts and PO Thomas Gould (*above, left & right*). 'A': first bomb penetrated gun platform. 'A1': its position between deck casing and pressure hull. 'B': position of second bomb on the casing. 'C': PO Gould stands in the hatch to which the first bomb was dragged. Off Crete, 16 February 1942.

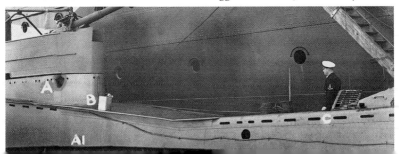

46 & 47. Pte Adam Wakenshaw (*left*) continued to serve his gun though very severely wounded. A later shell killed him. His wrecked 2-pdr is now in the Durham Light Infantry museum (*below*). Western Desert, 27 June 1942.

48 & 49. T/Lt-Col Henry Foote (*left*) led his last Matildas from an open turret, disregarding wounds and heavy fire. His example encouraged his exhausted crews and brought success. Libya, 13 June 1942.

50. *Above.* CSM Stanley Hollis won the first VC of the land invasion of Europe for single-handedly neutralising a sunken pillbox and a large bunker. Normandy, D-Day, 6 June 1944.

51. *Above, right.* A/Flt-Sgt Arthur Aaron was terribly injured on a bombing mission, by fire from another Stirling. He was posthumously honoured for his indomitable courage. Turin, Italy, 13 August 1943.

52 & 53. Rifleman Ganju Lama (*right*) single-handedly engaged three Japanese tanks. Though seriously wounded, he knocked out two of them (*below*). Burma, 12 June 1944.

54. *Above*. Lt Ian Fraser and A/LS James Magennis crippled a Japanese heavy cruiser at its moorings. After fitting the mines, they found their X-craft was stuck beneath the ship. Johore Straits, 31 July 1945.

55. *Right*. Lt-Col Herbert Jones gave his life to reinvigorate an assault, charging an Argentinian position almost alone. The objective was taken. Darwin, Falkland Islands, 28 May 1982.

56. *Left*. Pte Johnson Beharry was twice ambushed in Al Amarah, Iraq. His Warrior armoured vehicle was hit by RP grenades on both occasions, when as driver he displayed extreme gallantry. 1 May and 11 June 2004.

already been injured by a shell splinter, and, as bullets struck the ground about him, he calmly sat his horse and called down for volunteers to save the guns. Cpl George Nurse and six men responded, but more were needed. Three of Buller's ADCs rode forward, Capt Walter Congreve of the Rifle Brigade, Capt Harry Schofield, Royal Field Artillery, and Lt Freddy Roberts of the Kings Royal Rifles, only son of FM 'Bobs' Roberts, who had won his VC during the Indian Mutiny. Limbering up for parades was one thing. Under fire on wet ground with frightened horses was another. The limber, a large ammunition box perched the length of the axle on a single pair of high wheels, had to be manhandled back to the gun's heavy trail, which was then lifted and coupled to its rear. The six-horse team was hooked in to the limber's single pole-shaft in front. If a horse was hit, the equipage might be overturned by a thrashing team before the injured animal could be cut free and replaced.

The volunteers hooked teams into limbers and spurred out of the donga into a firestorm for the long gallop to the guns. Congreve recalled that 'Roberts was laughing and slapping his leg with his stick'. Moments later a shell burst under his horse and he lay mortally wounded. Congreve survived hits by four bullets. His horse took three more before falling 100yd short of the guns.

Schofield and Nurse took two limbers and miraculously reached the guns, selecting a pair well clear of dead horses. The spade-clamping gear of the first was jammed on the trail, preventing its hooking to a limber. They ran to another and limbered up. Schofield successfully galloped the gun back to the donga. Nurse ran back to the first gun, found the locking pin and coupled up with help from Pte George Ravenhill of the Royal Scots Fusiliers, one of the battery escort party. Ravenhill repeatedly left cover for subsequent recovery attempts. Nurse got his gun back to the donga. The Boer fire intensified as Buller dispatched further teams. All were shot to a halt. Capt Hamilton Reed of the 7th Battery brought up three fresh teams. Less than halfway to the guns five of his thirteen men were wounded and one killed, and thirteen of the twenty-one horses fell. Buller gave the order to retire. A night attempt would have meant holding back several exhausted battalions with further heavy loss. The ten remaining guns were abandoned. Meanwhile, Maj William Babtie of the Royal Army Medical Corps had reached the forward donga, his pony hit three times en route. He found many wounded and tended them all, coming under heavy fire whenever he showed himself. When the injured Congreve joined him, the two men braved the storm to bring in Roberts and other wounded.

Fathers and sons have both received the VC on only three occasions. By remarkable coincidence two of the recipients in this action are among those six names. Lt Frederick Roberts died two days later but was nevertheless awarded the Cross and so followed his father, the much-loved Field Marshal Lord Roberts, becoming the first father and son VCs. The gun Frederick had died to save was presented to Lord Roberts. Fourteen years later it bore the coffin at his funeral. Capt (later Lt-Gen) Walter Congreve VC became a corps commander in the First World War, losing a hand. His son Bt/Maj William La Touche Congreve of the Rifle Brigade was awarded a post-humous VC in France in July 1916, making them the second father and son holders of the Cross. William became the first officer to gain the VC, DSO and MC.

Well-earned VCs also went to Maj Babtie, Capt Schofield, Capt Reed, Cpl Nurse, and Pte Ravenhill. Schofield's Cross was delayed when Gen Buller commended his action but not the award of a VC, considering that Schofield was 'merely . . . acting under orders'. The War Office pointed out that the 1881 Warrant specified 'conspicuous bravery . . . in the presence of the enemy'. Pte George Ravenhill was the last recipient to forfeit his VC. His name was erased from the Register in August 1908 after he had served one month's imprisonment for theft of less than 6s worth (30p) of iron.

Korn Spruit, 31 March 1900

Maj Edmund Phipps-Hornby. Sgt Charles Parker. Gunner Isaac Lodge. Driver Horace Glasock. Lt Francis Maxwell

FM Lord Roberts was dispatched from London to take supreme command following the defeats at Colenso and elsewhere in 'Black Week'. The indomitable 'Colenso' action was repeated three months later at Korn Spruit. Common to both engagements was the poor judgement of senior commanders, the extraordinary gallantry of junior artillery officers and men and their escort troops, and the humiliating capture of near-sacred guns by Boer farmers.

The British marched into Bloemfontein, capital of the Orange Free State, on 18 March 1900. A fortnight later Brig-Gen R.G. Broadwood's expeditionary column of 1,700 men including 'Q' and 'W' Batteries of the Royal Horse Artillery and some ninety wagons was retiring to the capital following brushes with 1,100 Boer commandos. Early on the morning of the 31st, to the column's surprise, its bivouac came under heavy fire from Mauser and Martini-Henry rifles and two guns on the far bank of the Modder. Broadwood rashly decided to limber up and withdraw the whole column to Bushman's Kop, a hill several miles distant. He first dispatched the guns, 200 dismounted men, supply wagons and the refugees. No scouts went ahead.

Maj Edmund Phipps-Hornby's 'Q' Battery followed at a short distance. As they approached a ford in the Korn Spruit they saw the rest of the convoy thickly lining the bank 300yd ahead, and 'W' Battery drawing up alongside. A man ran back to tell Phipps-Hornby the detachment had been ambushed and taken prisoner. He ordered his battery to turn about. This brought a hail of bullets, which killed several horses. A gun overturned and was abandoned when the wheel horse was shot. The fusillade strengthened to a leaden firestorm as the remaining five 12pdrs were hauled to a ridge 1,150yd from the ford and began returning fire. After nearly three hours only Phipps-Hornby,

Sgt Charles Parker, a corporal and eight gunners remained in action of the original fifty-one officers and men. Driver Glasock recalled the ground was spurting with falling shot like the surface of a lake in heavy rain. Broadwood sent word to retire. Horses would have been felled in moments. Four guns and limbers were most bravely manhandled back with help from some of the Essex Regiment and were then galloped across two dry spruits to where the battery was re-forming. The fifth was abandoned after several fruitless attempts at recovery. Phipps-Hornby noticed how irrational men can become under such appalling conditions, some moving bent as in a gale – which of course it was – with a hand instinctively steadying the helmet. A gunner unthinkingly walked back to pick up the stick knocked out of his hand by a bullet. Sgt Parker had fought his gun alone for nearly an hour. When it was over he found bullet holes through his haversack, water bottle, helmet and boots, but he was untouched. Gen De Wet captured seven guns at Korn Spruit, taking 428 prisoners and 117 wagons. 'Q' Battery lost 33 killed or wounded and 7 missing.

The C-in-C judged the conduct of all ranks of 'Q' Battery so conspicuously gallant that he invoked Rule 13 of the VC Warrant for the first time since the Indian Mutiny. One officer, one NCO and two gunners or drivers were to be nominated by those of their peers who took part in the action. The balloted VCs went to Maj Phipps-Hornby, whose steady leadership and quick thinking avoided total disaster, Sgt Parker, Gunner Isaac Lodge, and Driver Horace Glasock, who was twice wounded and had six horses killed under him that day.

The fifth VC of the action was awarded on the intervention of the Queen. Lord Roberts had recommended the Cross for Lt Frank Maxwell of the Indian Staff Corps (attached to Roberts's Light Horse). He had gone out five times to help bring in two guns and three limbers, one of which he and another ran back by hand. Maxwell also attempted to recover the last gun before it was abandoned. The WO considered four Crosses more than adequate for the Korn Spruit action, refusing to recommend the award. There it might have rested had Maxwell's sister not written to a Mrs South on 16 October expressing the family's disappointment that this was the second time her brother had been recommended for the Cross and not received it. Presumably Mrs South was a lady at court, as Queen Victoria's Private Secretary wrote on 10 November to inform the Military Secretary that 'Her Majesty cannot help thinking that if this really is the case his claim to the coveted honour is a strong one'. The case was reviewed and a recommendation submitted to the Palace on 26 February 1901. It was one of the first VCs to be approved by King Edward VII. The Queen had passed away five weeks before. Maxwell commanded a battalion of the Middlesex Regiment in France in the First World War, gaining a bar to his DSO before he was killed in action near Ypres in September 1917.

The Korn Spruit action brought a suggestion in December 1901 that, when a unit such as a battery participated in a ballot, the battery itself should be granted some permanent insignia, perhaps a cloth badge bearing a facsimile of the Cross. The Assistant Adjutant General suggested alternatively that the emblem of the VC be added to the Colours, or worn by senior NCOs where there was no Colour. The Adjutant General rightly ruled that 'the VC . . . should be a purely personal distinction'.

Individual Acts of Gallantry

L/Cpl John Mackay. Tpr Horace Ramsden. Sgt Horace Martineau. Pte James Pitts. Pte Robert Scott

L/Cpl John Frederick Mackay, 1st Battalion The Gordon Highlanders, nearly became the first man to win a Bar to his VC. On 20 May 1900 during an action at Doorncop near Johannesburg, Mackay repeatedly rushed forward under a withering fire at short range to attend wounded comrades while remaining fully exposed. In one instance he carried an injured man across fireswept ground to the shelter of a boulder. By some miracle he came through all this unscathed. He was recommended for the Cross by Lord Roberts on 25 June. The submission went to the Queen on 4 August and was gazetted on the 10th. Meanwhile Mackay had been recommended for the Bar for an exploit performed on 11 July at Wolverkrantz near Krugersdorp. After the slightly notorious case of Lt Henry Marsham Havelock of Indian Mutiny fame, the War Office was committed to extremely rigid interpretation of the Warrant for submissions for the Bar. Because Mackay's initial recommendation was not approved before the date of his second exploit, he was deemed not to have held the Cross at that time and had no entitlement to a Bar. He ended his Army career as a lieutenant-colonel.

*   *   *

Many Crosses went to men who risked their lives to tend and bring in the wounded. After Maj Charles Gough's rescue of his injured brother in 1857 during the Indian Mutiny, the second such brotherly act occurred at Game Tree near Mafeking on 26 December 1899. When the order to retire was given, Tpr Horace Ramsden of the Protectorate Regiment, a scratch corps hastily raised for the protection of Mafeking, saw his brother shot through both legs only 10yd from the Boer trenches. Ramsden defiantly returned to pick him up and carry him nearly 800yd under heavy fire the whole way, resting at intervals until he met others to help carry his brother to safety. He got away without a scratch, unlike Sgt Horace Martineau of the same regiment who was struggling nearby to bring in wounded Cpl Le Camp. Martineau was hit three times, half carrying and half dragging Le Camp until he collapsed. His devotion cost him his arm. Ramsden and Martineau both gained VCs for their selfless gallantry. Their unit was one of sixty or seventy corps raised in Africa that joined the British Army in the field.

Ramsden remained in the Cape until his death in 1948. Martineau was commissioned, later moving to New Zealand.

*   *   *

The stubborn resistance of Ptes James Pitts and Robert Scott of the Manchester Regiment typified the resource and determination of isolated individuals and small groups whose VCs were earned when command and communication were lost in the heat of battle. Both gained Crosses after holding their post under fire for fifteen hours. The 1st Battalion was manning a picket line at Caesar's Camp, a key ridge along the southern defences of Ladysmith, when the Boers launched a powerful night assault to take the position on 6 January 1900. Its only defence works were a chain of sangars – heaped stone enclosures – unconnected by trenches. Surrounding scrub had not been cleared of cover. The Transvaalers stormed up and over the ridge, taking the Manchesters in the rear and cutting them down in swathes. Without food or water, Pitt and Scott held their post under constant and often heavy fire that night and throughout the following day. The sangars to their left and left rear were occupied by the enemy, leaving them as the last surviving defenders. Scott was wounded in the action.

OTHER VC ACTIONS, 1900–1913

CHINA. THE BOXER REBELLION, 1900

Capt Lewis Halliday RM

The Boxer uprising in Peking and elsewhere in 1900 threatened death to all foreigners and Christians in response to increasing foreign penetration of China. The walled quarter in Peking housing the legations became a refuge for some 3,500 foreigners and Chinese Christians. They were besieged for fifty-five days by Imperial troops and 30,000 Boxer rebels until an

Anglo-American force of 18,000 reached the city on 14 August. The Imperial Court fled, later agreeing terms permitting permanent foreign garrisoning of the legations and along the railway to the coast, and paying a substantial indemnity.

Troops and rebels had burst into the packed British compound on 24 June and kept up a hot rifle fire from outbuildings. The legation was defended by fifty men of the Royal Marine Light Infantry commanded by Capt Lewis Halliday, who led a sortie of twenty Marines to clear the enemy before reinforcements could reach them. They rushed the buildings, where Halliday was immediately shot point blank, the ball fracturing his left shoulder and penetrating a lung. It should have left him in agony on the threshold, but there were women and children in the Residency and Cawnpore was not forgotten. He fought on, shooting three enemy before calling his men to carry on and not mind him. He walked back alone to avoid reducing their strength. Capt Halliday was awarded the VC for his courageous leadership and example. He ended his service as Colonel Commandant of the Royal Marines, dying in 1966.

NIGERIA, KANO–SOKOTO EXPEDITION, 1903

Capt Wallace Wright

Confronted with French ambitions in West Africa, the British declared a protectorate over Northern and Southern Nigeria in 1900. Abolition of the slave trade conducted by Muslim emirates in the territory became an early priority. Those who resisted were raided by the West African Frontier Force. In 1903 Sir Frederick Lugard the High Commissioner dispatched 700 men to invade the mud-walled city of Kano.

Newly promoted Capt Wallace Duffield Wright of the Queen's Royal West Surrey Regiment, serving with the Northern Nigeria Regiment, found himself with one officer and forty-four men facing a horde of advancing warriors. In the ensuing confrontation on 26 February his party resisted repeated charges by some 1,000 horsemen and 2,000 spear-carrying tribesmen on foot. Wright's determined leadership and good fire discipline turned each assault. Two very long hours later the enemy fell back in good order after suffering heavy losses, pursued by the gallant party until they were in full retreat. Wallace Wright received the VC, later serving on the Western Front from 1916, eventually as Brigadier General commanding an Infantry Brigade. He was mentioned in dispatches five times.

TIBET, 1903–1904

Lt John Grant

A hair-raising action in Tibet on 6 July 1904 gained the VC for Lt (later Col) John Duncan Grant of the 8th Gurkha Rifles. The Russians sought control of Tibet, thus threatening India's frontier. When British negotiations with Tibet's rulers failed in 1903, an armed mission set out with 1,100 troops to secure cooperation. Agreement was reached after Brig-Gen Macdonald's force took Tibet's near impregnable Gyantse Jong fortress, whose citadel containing several thousand troops crowned a near-precipitous cliff. A preliminary artillery bombardment blew its magazine and eventually breached the curtain wall.

The breach was approachable only by climbing a narrow rising ledge across the rockface on hands and knees in single file. Lt Grant led the storming party under fire from the wall above and from flanking towers. Next behind him was Havildar (Sgt) Karbir Pun. Rocks were dropped on them by the enemy and there was little cover. Nearing the top both men were wounded and toppled back, the Havildar falling 30ft. Despite their injuries, they completed the climb. With covering fire from below, Grant was first man in as the party successfully penetrated the fortress. By 6pm it was taken. Lt Grant received the Cross and Havildar Karbir Pun its then equivalent, the Indian Order of Merit. The brave Gurkha was later commissioned, and died in 1910. Grant served with distinction in the First World War and retired in 1947 as Colonel of the 10th Gurkha Rifles. He died aged 90 in 1967.

* * *

Twelve VCs in all were gained in the above engagements and others in the Gambia, Somaliland and Nigeria between 1900 and 1913. John Grant's VC was the 522nd to be awarded, and the last before the First World War.

6

The First World War,
1914–1918

It's strange dying, Blake old boy – unlike anything
one has ever done before, like one's first solo.

*(The mortally wounded 2/Lt William Bernard
Rhodes-Moorhouse RFC to Flt Cdr Maurice Blake,
Merville, France, 27 April 1915; Rhodes-Moorhouse
was awarded the VC posthumously)*

Agunshot on the streets of Sarajevo on 28 June 1914
triggered the coming deaths in battle of over seven million
young men of many nations, the flower of their generation. The
assassination of Archduke Franz Ferdinand, heir to the Austrian
throne, caused rival alliances across Europe to exchange
ultimatums and order mobilisation. Germany invaded Belgium
on 4 August. London's ultimatum to Berlin followed and was
rejected. Britain declared war at 11 p.m. that night.

Important lessons had been learned since the Boer War. The
infantry tactics, training and battledress of Britain's all-
professional Army emphasised fieldcraft, concealment and
delivery of very high rates of fire. The infantryman's regulation
fifteen aimed rounds per minute with the new clip-loading .303
Lee-Enfield magazine rifle was unattainable by the huge
conscript armies of the major European powers. Like Britain,
they planned and trained for wars of manoeuvre. No high
command contemplated, let alone prepared for, siege war. The
Royal Navy had expanded its fleet of Dreadnought all-big-gun
capital ships and enthusiastically adopted new technologies, fire

control and weapons systems, though it still lacked a proper naval staff. The tank weapon was wholly developed by Winston Churchill's Navy, the Army having rejected the concept in February 1915. Virtually no cooperation or joint planning existed between the two Services until well into 1915.

Between August 1914 and the Armistice in November 1918 a total of 626 VCs and 2 Bars were awarded, some 180 of them posthumously. The overwhelming majority of Crosses, more than 500, were gained in France and Belgium.

Mons, 22–23 August 1914

Lt Maurice Dease. Pte Sidney Godley. L/Cpl Charles Jarvis. Capt Theodore Wright. Cpl Charles Garforth

Sir John French led a small, tough and highly professional British Expeditionary Force across the Channel and up into Belgium; four infantry divisions and five brigades of cavalry totalling 80,000 men, 315 field guns and 30,000 horses. On 22 August Lt-Gen Sir Horace Smith-Dorrien's II Corps dug in along the line of the Mons–Condé canal running east–west on the left flank of the French armies. A British cavalry squadron killed three Uhlans in the BEF's first engagement of the war that day. Five VCs were won over the next twenty-four hours when Gen von Kluck threw six divisions against Smith-Dorrien's line.

The battle on the 23rd was hottest where a section of the canal looped north round Mons to form a salient. Its crossings at that point were held by the 4th Battalion Royal Fusiliers. Capt Ashburner's 'C' Company lay beside the canal's Nimy railway bridge. Lt Maurice Dease had positioned its two machine guns on the buttresses to either side. After a preliminary bombardment, four battalions of German infantry advanced on the bridge in a dense mass. They were met with a '15 rounds rapid' blast of rifle fire, which, with the Vickers machine guns, flattened the leading sections. The rest withdrew to regroup, prisoners later refusing to believe they had not been struck by several batteries of machine guns. 'C' Company was taking the weight of six German battalions at this point. Their next assault, this time in extended order, was checked but not halted. Dease's exposed machine guns behind shingle-filled flour sacks became the focus of heavy fire, killing or wounding successive crews. Dease controlled them from a trench 50yd behind the bridge, repeatedly joining the guns when either stopped firing. He was hit in the leg while attending the first to be silenced, and wounded in the side as he crawled to the other. After a brief rest he insisted on returning to his guns, where he was struck down by another bullet as he directed fire from the centre of the bridge. Mortally wounded, Maurice Dease was dragged to shelter.

By the time orders came to pull back, both machine-gun positions were unmanned and piled with the dead. Pte Sidney Godley volunteered to give covering fire for the withdrawal. He cleared the right-hand machine gun of three bodies and emptied belt after belt under intense fire. Shell fragments penetrated his back and later a bullet struck his head. Lt Pease helped for a time, until he was killed. After two hours, with all ammunition fired off and still disregarding his wounds, Godley disabled his gun and threw it into the canal before crawling to seek aid. He was captured soon afterwards. On Christmas Day 1914 the prison camp's officers invited him to dine with them, chivalry being not quite dead. They recognised that his VC equated to their equally revered Pour le Mérite

Orders to blow eight bridges were issued to 57 Field Company Royal Engineers. It proved impossible with only one exploder and little time. The Jemappes bridge was prepared with immense courage by L/Cpl Charles Jarvis. As his intentions became clear, he drew fire for ninety minutes while laying slabs of guncotton, tamping them with wet clay and wiring up. He then went to find Capt Theodore Wright, who led the demolition teams, moving between them under constant fire despite a bad head wound. Wright refused the Corporal's offer to bandage it, ordering him back to the bridge to await his arrival with the exploder and leads. Jarvis was one of the last to withdraw after a fruitless wait there. He never claimed to have blown the Jemappes bridge, as his VC citation infers, but it makes clear that he did destroy 'a bridge'. Wright too earned the Cross for twice attempting to connect leads to demolish a bridge under heavy fire despite his wound, and for his gallantry at Vailly on 14 September as the 5th Cavalry Brigade crossed a pontoon bridge under shell fire. He was seen patching deck sections as they were hit, and putting down straw to steady hooves. Theo Wright was killed shortly afterwards when helping wounded men into shelter.

Lt Dease gained the first VC of the war and Pte Godley the second. After VCs for Capt Wright and L/Cpl Jarvis, the fifth man to gain one that day was Cpl Charles Garforth, 15th Hussars, whose Cross covered three engagements. His troop was nearly surrounded while fighting a rearguard action near Harmignies. It was halted by a wire fence enfiladed by Maxim fire. Dismounting, Garforth entered the bullet-swept zone and cut a way through, enabling the troop to gallop off. On 6 September, as his patrol withdrew under fierce fire, he went back to free Sgt Scatterfield lying trapped under his wounded horse. Next day he used his rifle on an MG position, drawing its fire to enable dismounted Sgt Lewis to reach cover. Charles Garforth was captured in October, later making three attempts to escape.

Nery, 1 September 1914

Capt Edward Bradbury. Battery Sgt-Maj George Dorrell. Sgt David Nelson

The epic gallantry of 'L' Battery, Royal Horse Artillery, typified the determination and guts of the BEF during the Allied retreat towards Paris. 'Stick to your guns' is a familiar exhortation with never a truer example than theirs. Capt Edward Bradbury's battery was attached to the 1st Cavalry Brigade forming the rearguard of III Corps. His gunners and a squadron of the

Queen's Bays had bivouacked after dark on 31 August in the village of Nery, 12 miles south-west of Compiègne. Next morning in low mist they were attacked by six German cavalry regiments with artillery support. Fire was concentrated on the battery, whose teams were harnessing up for the march but not yet hooked into limbers. As men strove to bring their guns to bear without the horses they were engulfed in an inferno of shell and rifle fire. Within two minutes almost the entire battery lay dead or wounded and every horse was killed.

One 13pdr remained operational. Bradbury called the few survivors together to crew it. Lt Giffard was wounded four times before reaching them. Lt John Campbell, Lt John Mundy, Battery Sgt-Maj George Dorrell, Sgt David Nelson, Gunner Darbyshire and Driver Osborne also responded. A crew under pressure and firing over open sights could maintain a rate of twenty rounds a minute, but, with no horses left to bring up an ammunition wagon, every shell had to be fetched by hand through a smoking blizzard of steel. Bradbury was directing fire early on when his leg was blown off by a shell. Propping himself against the trail he continued to give encouragement despite his massive injury until a second shell killed him instantly. Sgt Dorrell took over, Sgt Nelson also remaining with the gun though severely wounded. Lt Mundy rose to observe the fall of shot, shouting 'they can't hit me'. He coolly continued to direct fire until a shell took away part of his leg, from which he later died. The survivors fired off two wagonloads of ammunition. Lt Campbell was killed carrying the last round. Four of the enemy's eight guns were destroyed by the 13pdr. The remainder were silenced by 'I' Battery, which had providentially arrived. Bradbury's battered gun now stands in London's Imperial War Museum, its muzzle rim driven back by a German shell. Sgt-Maj Dorrell and Sgt Nelson received VCs and Capt Bradbury was honoured with a posthumous Cross. Lt Giffard was awarded France's Order of Merit. Gunner Darbyshire and Driver Osborne were recommended for the Distinguished Conduct Medal.

The First Battle of Ypres, 20 October–17 November 1914

Lt Arthur Martin-Leake. Lt James Brooke. Sepoy Khudadad Khan.

The magnificent but very costly Anglo/French stand at Ypres ended Germany's drive for a major breakthrough and secured the Channel ports, vital to the BEF's existence.

Lt Arthur Martin-Leake was the first of only three men to gain a Bar to the VC. As a 27-year-old Surgeon-Captain with the South African Constabulary during the Boer War at Vlakfontein in the Transvaal, he had entered the firing line on 8 February 1902 to attend a wounded man under very heavy fire from a large force of Boer commandos. When he moved on to help mortally wounded Lt Abraham, he was shot three times. Martin-Leake continued this work for a considerable period in complete disregard of the danger, and pain of his wounds in arm and thigh, until finally collapsing. He refused water until the other wounded had been served. King George V decorated him with the Cross, but it had been a close-run thing. FM Lord Kitchener had vetoed the recommendation, proposing a DSO in the belief that Martin-Leake was only doing his duty. It was the same reasoning that Gen Buller had applied to Capt Schofield's VC after Colenso. Kitchener was overruled, on the intervention of Lord Brodrick, Secretary of State at the War Office. The question 'was he doing more than his duty' was misplaced, because every man's duty was to do his utmost.

Martin-Leake joined the Royal Army Medical Corps in September 1914 on attachment to the 5th Field Ambulance with the rank of Lieutenant. Between 29 October and 8 November during the critical First Battle of Ypres he repeatedly braved fireswept ground to recover the wounded lying close to the enemy's trenches. It was a rare courage that steeled him and others like him to leave the security of a trench and cross the killing zone alone to within a few metres of the enemy before crawling the entire way back dragging an injured man, and repeating this for days on end. Lt Martin-Leake was decorated by the King at Windsor before returning to France.

It was only when Hancocks were instructed to add a Bar to his Cross that it was realised no design for one existed. Hancocks sketched two suggestions. Both show a second laureated bar set a little above, and closely resembling, the suspender of the Cross. In one version the ribbon appears to finish at the upper bar, which is connected to the suspender by small links. In the other the ribbon clearly goes right to the suspender as usual, with a circular laurel wreath mounted to straddle bar and suspender. Forwarding them for decision to Maj-Gen Sir Frederick Robb the Military Secretary, Lt-Col B.R. James noted: 'The circular wreath seems neither beautiful nor necessary.' Robb agreed: 'I think the bar should be an exact copy of the existing one.' Hancocks were instructed accordingly: 'the dates of the acts of bravery to be engraved on the back'.

The British Medical Association awarded Martin-Leake its Gold medal in 1915. He ended the war as a lieutenant-colonel commanding a casualty clearing station with 1st Army, before resuming his medical work with the Bengal–Nagpur Railway.

The quick thinking of Lt James Otho Brooke of the Gordon Highlanders prevented a German breakthrough near Gheluvelt on 29 October when an Allied counter-attack could not have been mounted. The 7th Division had been hit by a greatly superior force. At this critical moment Brooke was sent by his colonel with a message from one end of the line to the other. On his way he saw the enemy penetrating a section. Gathering 80–100 men he led them in two charges through heavy rifle and machine-gun fire, successfully driving the Germans back, regaining a lost trench and forestalling a serious breach. Brooke then consolidated the position, repeatedly exposing himself to intense fire. He was killed while seeing to the strengthening of his defences. One officer recalled that Brooke twice left the trench and doubled behind a wrecked house to send a message for support. He had to cover 25yd each way in the open as bullets spattered red dust from the walls and rubble-strewn ground. Lt Brooke, a regular officer, was awarded a posthumous VC. At Sandhurst he had captained the Shooting Eight, tied for the Saddle, was Senior Colour-Sergeant of the College, and had won the Sword of Honour. He was one of the last of the magnificent regular British Army that was virtually wiped out at Ypres after so much valiant fighting in Flanders.

At Hollebeke two days later, Sepoy (Pte) Khudadad Khan became the first native soldier of the Indian Army to be awarded the VC. Although a Pathan, he was a member of the 129th Duke of Connaught's Own Baluchis. The regiment had faced the full fury of the German assault that day. He and his officer were severely wounded in heavy shelling that had killed the rest of his machine-gun detachment and smashed one of its two guns. Sepoy Khudadad courageously continued to work the other to good effect. When the position was rushed, he was left for dead, but managed to crawl away and escape with his life. The King presented him with his VC a month later as he lay in a field hospital. He survived the war, dying in Pakistan in 1971. With the end of the Indian Empire in 1947 the VC was closed to all Indian troops save the Brigade of Gurkhas, which became part of the British Army.

In the Trenches, 1914–1915

Lt Philip Neame. Lt Edward Bellew. Rifleman William Mariner (b. William Wignall). Sgt John Carmichael

No army was prepared for the trench warfare that followed. New tactics and weapons had to be developed. Munitions production under Gen Stanley von Donop, the Master General of Ordnance, remained a shambles. The 'shells scandal' forced the Army to hand over all design and production to Lloyd George's newly created Ministry of Munitions in May 1915. Christopher Addison, Parliamentary Secretary at the Ministry, discovered that every machine gun was taking the War Office eight months to produce. A minimum of 50,000 hand grenades was required daily at that time, against an output rated 'negligible'.

In the trenches men devised their own hand-thrown 'bombs'. Jam tins with a primitive wick fuse were packed with explosive and metal scrap. Lt Philip Neame of 15 Field Company RE, wiry and a crack shot, was in the line at Neuve Chapelle the day after a successful attack on 18 December 1914. Hearing that the West Yorkshires were in difficulties holding a newly captured position, Neame went up alone to reconnoitre. He found a sergeant and two men isolated in the most forward German traverse. They were the only survivors of a bombing party that had held the trench against fierce German counter-attack. The German bombs (grenades) outranged the BEF's home-made version, whose fuses were damp and difficult to light.

Just then another raid began, bombs raining down from further along the trench. A soldier behind Neame was killed, and more were dying in the next two traverses. Neame grabbed a jam-tin bomb, shortened the fuse with a pocket knife to reduce its 4-second delay, and, in the absence of slow-burning fusees, he struck a matchbox across a match head held tight against the clean-cut fuse end, before hurling it over. It silenced that bay, but further attacks followed at intervals from two directions. For the next forty-five minutes Neame prepared and threw more bombs, as unseen raiders were heard nearby. A German machine gun opened up, missing him each time his head and shoulders emerged to hurl a bomb. He contributed greatly towards checking the assault. Lt Gen Philip Neame VC held high commands in North Africa in the Second World War before capture with Gen Sir Richard O'Connor in Cyrenaica in 1941. The two escaped from Italy in 1943. Neame was Colonel Commandant RE from 1945 to 1955.

The first Canadian VC of the war was won by Lt Edward Bellew of the 7th Canadian Infantry Battalion, British Columbia Regiment, during the second battle of Ypres in April 1915. Von Württemberg's Fourth Army released chlorine gas, opening a 5-mile gap in the line on the 22nd. Ypres lay before them. The break was plugged with twelve Canadian and nine British battalions, all severely weakened, facing forty-two German battalions with a five-to-one superiority in guns. At 04.00 on the 24th von Württemberg launched a gas attack on the Canadians, whose only protection were handkerchiefs, towels and cotton bandoliers soaked in water or urine.

Battalion machine-gun officer Bellew had sited his two Vickers on high ground, where the enemy's assault broke in full force, exposing the Canadian flank. Reinforcements never reached them. Under intense fire and in a haze of gas, with no further assistance in sight, the 7th retired to a new position under covering fire from Bellew's guns. His detachment stood firm and kept up fire until a heavy shell killed all save Bellew, who was wounded. Recovering somewhat, he fired off the remaining belts. In the pause he was rushed, but snatching a rifle he emptied it before reversing it to smash his gun. Bellew's captors sentenced him to death for continuing to resist after the surrender of elements of his unit. He faced a firing squad against the wall of Staden church, the officer in charge relenting only at the last moment in face of his protests. Sir John French later praised the Canadians for saving the day. Lt Bellew was released from captivity early in 1919. He learned of his award when the announcement appeared in a Vancouver newspaper on his return home. Later he became involved in survey and construction work in British Columbia.

Many sorts and conditions of men gained the VC. Rifleman William Mariner of the King's Royal Rifle Corps was in fact William Wignall from Chorley, well known in police circles and seemingly an ex-convict. It must have been on re-enlistment with his old battalion in August 1914 that he assumed the name of Mariner with no questions asked. He showed courage of a very high order the following May in volunteering to cross no man's land alone to eliminate a German machine-gun post that had inflicted heavy casualties on his battalion near Cambrin. Under cover of a violent thunderstorm on the night of the 22nd the slightly built 32-year-old penetrated the German wire and reached the parapet fronting the machine-gun emplacement. There he lobbed a bomb through the fire-slot, afterwards hearing groans and the sounds of men dispersing. A quarter of an hour later Mariner heard the enemy returning. Risking discovery, he climbed to the other side of the emplacement and lobbed a second bomb. It brought down heavy fire on the wire behind him where he was thought to be. He lay low for a while until all went quiet before making his way back to the 2nd Battalion's trench. William Mariner was awarded the Cross for his exceptional courage and success. On 1 July the following year he became one of the 19,240 British and Commonwealth dead on the first day of the Battle of the Somme.

A different sort of courage inspired Sgt John Carmichael of the North Staffordshires. During trench-digging at Zwarteleen near Hill 60 in Belgium on 8 September 1917, a buried grenade was struck and activated. With 3–4 seconds to react, Carmichael rushed over and covered it with his helmet before standing on it. He was blown out of the trench and severely injured. Had he thrown the grenade over the parapet, it would, he knew, have killed members of a working party. His willing self-sacrifice for his comrades was in the highest traditions of the Cross that he gained. John Carmichael died in 1977.

The Air War's First VC, 26 April, 1915

2/Lt William Barnard Rhodes-Moorhouse RFC

The young airmen who went 'over the top' almost daily in the First World War and whose life expectancy on the Western Front sometimes fell to two or three sorties, gained nineteen VCs, four of them posthumously. 2/Lt William Rhodes-Moorhouse was the first air VC. He left Cambridge in 1909 aged 22 to race cars and learn to fly. In 1911 he co-designed the Radley-Moorhouse monoplane, won around £1,000 at a San Francisco air race – also becoming the first to fly through the archways of the Golden Gate Bridge – and gained his pilot's licence back home. He enlisted in the Royal Flying Corps in August 1914 and after much pleading was sent to France the following March to join 2 Squadron at Merville. They were flying reliable but unimpressive BE2b two-seat types, the underpowered Renault engine obliging them to shed an observer to compensate for the bomb load.

The days following the first devastating German gas attack on 22 April 1915 and General von Württemberg's breakthrough to Saint-Julien on the 24th were most critical. Ypres was threatened, and huge efforts were made to sustain RFC air reconnaissance and bombing operations. German troop concentrations in the Ghent area on the 26th brought orders for 2 Squadron to dispatch four aircraft to attack rail communications at Roubaix, Turcoing and the junction at Courtrai. Rhodes-Moorhouse was assigned the junction. He took off at 15.05 for the 35-minute solo flight in No. 687, a 100lb high-explosive bomb suspended beneath the centre section of the fuselage. His familiar No. 492 was under repair after damage received on a photo recce flight on the 16th. Flt Cdr Maurice Blake had advised bombing from just below cloud cover but had left the decision to Rhodes-Moorhouse, who chose a shallow dive to 300ft on final approach to the target. It exposed him to ground fire from hundreds of rifles, augmented by a Maxim in the church belfry, which opened up point blank as he levelled off and steadied, before dropping the bomb accurately on lines west of the station. MG fire ripped across the cockpit, tearing his thigh. Soon afterwards a bullet cut open his abdomen and another damaged his hand. Rhodes-Moorhouse dropped to 100ft to coax a little more speed. In great pain, shocked and weakening from loss of blood, he nursed his shattered aircraft back to Merville.

Historian Peter Cooksley records that Air Mechanic Percy Butcher helped remove Rhodes-Moorhouse from the cockpit, later recalling that it was so awash with blood that he had expected to find a severed limb there. The mortally wounded pilot insisted on making his report before receiving medical attention. William Rhodes-Moorhouse asked to be buried in England, telling Maurice Blake that dying was a strange business, like flying one's first solo. At about 14.30 hours next day he bravely flew his last and longest solo. The ashes of his son, Flying Officer William Henry Rhodes-Moorhouse DFC, killed in action during the Battle of Britain, are interred beside his father at Parnham House, the family's Dorset home.

Gallipoli, April–December 1915

At the end of 1914 Russia called on the Western Allies to open a 'second front' against Turkey to relieve pressure on its armies in the Caucasus. Winston Churchill at the Admiralty proposed a naval assault to drive Turkey out of the war and open a supply route to Russia via the Black Sea. Kitchener and the government approved, but an attempt to force the Dardanelles passage by naval attack alone failed in March 1915. The Gallipoli peninsula was accordingly invaded on 25 April by the Royal Naval Division, the Anzac (Australia and New Zealand) Corps, and British and French soldiers, 75,000 in all, led by Maj-Gen Sir Ian Hamilton. They faced 84,000 expectant and well-prepared Turkish troops. Despite Hamilton's weak command structure, bad communications and some instances of poor leadership ashore, a foothold was gained by nightfall, but at terrible cost. The campaign stalled and became a strategic irrelevance. Ironically its greatest success was a superbly planned withdrawal at the end of the year. British and Commonwealth casualties totalled 205,000, and French 47,000.

Altogether 39 VCs are attributable to the Dardanelles campaign on land, at sea and in the air, 11 of which were gained by the Royal Navy, 9 by the Australian Imperial Force and 1 each by the Royal Flying Corps and the New Zealand Expeditionary Force.

'V' Beach, 25 April 1915

Cdr A/Capt Edward Unwin RN. Seaman William Williams RNR. Midshipman George Drewry RNR. Midshipman Wilfred Malleson RN. Sub-Lt Arthur Tisdall RNR. Seaman George Samson RNR

Allied landings on the Gallipoli peninsula began at dawn from a fleet of 200 transports. Of the six beaches stormed, resistance on four was slight to non-existent, but 'V' and 'W' beaches on either side of Cape Helles were well-prepared, and V Beach especially was a death trap. A/Capt Edward Unwin commanded the *River Clyde*, a collier adapted to disgorge some 1,500 troops through large holes cut in her sides when she was driven ashore on 'V' beach. Lighters secured on either side of the vessel could be run out and lashed end to end as a landing pier if necessary. She also towed five strings of open boats packed with Dublin Fusiliers, the first to go ashore, to support the disembarkation. Machine guns on her upper deck would provide covering fire.

River Clyde's landing proved disastrous. As she grounded, she met devastating machine-gun and pom pom fire from concealed positions in the surrounding hills. The Fusiliers were slaughtered. Those who leapt from the boats became entangled in barbed wire laid on the seabed, and died there. Troops aboard the ship who tried to get ashore across the lighters fared little better. Unwin waded out with Seaman Bill Williams to secure the inshore lighter to a rock on the beach, the surface of the sea around them jumping with bullet strikes. They joined Midshipman George Drewry, who had to go back aboard to fetch a longer rope. As Unwin and Williams waited chest deep for fifty minutes in the lee of the barge, Williams was hit and died in Unwin's arms. Once secured, the lighters quickly became clogged with bodies as disembarking troops ran the gauntlet of murderous shot. An RNAS pilot reported that the sea off 'V' beach 'was absolutely red with blood'.

Bullets eventually severed lashings and the lighters separated. Drewry, still on the inshore craft and with a shrapnel wound to the head, jumped overboard with a line between his teeth and swam to the other. Again, the rope was too short. Seeing Drewry's strength failing, Midshipman Wilfred Malleson, aged 18, ran to the breach, dived over and resecured the lighters. Once more they were shot apart. Malleson made two more brave but unsuccessful attempts to rope them together. Meanwhile Unwin had been working in the water like a Trojan despite his fifty-one years. Three times wounded, he returned briefly to his ship before taking charge of a boat and making several journeys to rescue wounded men from the shallows. Throughout that night his voice was heard giving orders above the continuing noise of gunfire.

Some 200 surviving troops on shore was the limit of the day's advance. About 1,000 remained aboard awaiting nightfall. The beach was crowded with injured men, many suffering multiple wounds. Their cries drifted back to the ship, compelling newly commissioned Sub-Lt Arthur Tisdall to push a boat ahead of him and make for the shoreline, calling for others to help. LS James Malia responded at once, and the two successfully made two near-suicidal trips to bring off the wounded. Other helpers joined them for three more journeys under Tisdall's command. Meanwhile Seaman George Samson had remained on the lighters throughout, tending the wounded and assisting officers with the lashings. He was hit many times, later returning to England with twelve pieces of metal still in his body.

VCs for their sustained gallantry went to Cdr A/Capt Unwin, Sub-Lt Tisdall, Midshipman Drewry, Midshipman Malleson and Seamen Williams and Samson. LS Malia was awarded the CGM. Tisdall fell in action two weeks later. Unwin, Drewry, Malleson and Samson survived the war. Malleson became a captain and served in the Second World War, dying in 1975. Ironically, Samson was later presented with a white feather –

a token of cowardice – by a stranger as he walked in civilian dress to a public reception in his honour.

Lone Pine Trenches, 7–9 August 1915

Pte Leonard Keysor. Capt Alfred Shout

The taking and holding of Lone Pine Trenches further up the peninsular typified the fighting spirit of the hard-pressed Anzacs, with only 15 or 20yd separating the opposing trenches. They gained seven VCs in three days of almost continuous hand-to-hand fighting until the Turks withdrew.

Among those so honoured was Pte Leonard Keysor of the 1st Battalion (New South Wales) Australian Imperial Force, who proved a deadly bomb-thrower. He was in his element, also throwing back incoming grenades or smothering them with a well-directed sandbag or greatcoat. When the enemy shortened fuses, he relished catching them in the air as if he was on Sydney's cricket ground, and hurling them back. Though twice wounded, he refused to leave, instead volunteering to throw grenades for another company that had lost all its bombers. Keysor successfully carried out this vital and hazardous work for 50 hours almost non-stop.

Capt Alfred Shout, also of the 1st Battalion, had earlier distinguished himself at Gallipoli when on 27 April he led a bayonet charge for which he received the Military Cross. On 9 August he led a small party into the head of a strongly defended Turkish communication trench running well to the enemy's rear. Shout charged along it, throwing four bombs and killing eight defenders before clearing the first sap. They ran on, the men shooting round every traverse as Shout laughed, joked and bombed, all the time under heavy retaliatory fire. They reached a point where it seemed wise to halt and build a barricade to secure their gains. Shout lit three bombs together in an exuberant moment of madness, intending to throw the lot in quick succession to drive the enemy well back while the men worked. He hurled the first, but the second or third exploded as it left his hand, shattering it and most of his other hand, destroying an eye and causing other injuries. Remaining conscious, he drank tea, talked cheerfully and sent his wife a message, but he was sinking and died two days later. Capt Shout was awarded a posthumous VC.

Maj T.E. Lawrence and the VC

The charismatic Maj T.E. Lawrence had rallied the Arab revolt against the Turks, transforming the Arabs' 'loose shower of sparks' into a blow torch that burned up Turkish military manpower and resources. The fall of Akaba in August 1917 brought him high commendations, especially from those officers with long experience of the Arabs who had seen his achievements at first hand. The Staff in Cairo was more impressed with Lawrence's secret activities in Syria. Gen Sir Reginald Wingate, High Commissioner for Egypt, reported Lawrence's journey into Syria as 'little short of marvellous' and noted that the Turks had put a price of £5,000 on his head. Wingate recommended 'immediate award of the Victoria Cross . . . this recommendation is amply justified by [Lawrence's] skill, pluck and endurance'.

The recommendation was rejected in London, as Lawrence's actions were not witnessed by two other British officers. This was not required by the VC Warrant, but was a prevailing 'domestic arrangement on the part of the Field Marshal in France' (Col Graham, War Office, 30 August 1918). Lawrence later refused a DSO. He was nevertheless appointed a Companion of the Order of the Bath and promoted to major. He was embittered by his enforced role in the betrayal of his promises to the Arabs, and despised the awards that followed. Had he gained the Cross he might have returned it.

The Battle of the Somme, 1 July–18 November 1916

Pte William McFadzean. Sgt James Turnbull. T/Lt-Col Roland Boys Bradford

For nearly four years Germany's *Maschinengewehr '08* Maxims dominated the battlefield. They did terrible execution on 1 July 1916 and in the following weeks. Lt-Gen Sir Douglas Haig had succeeded Sir John French in December 1915. Haig's largely British offensive beside the Somme river was mounted primarily to aid France by relieving pressure on Verdun, where eventually some 420,000 Frenchmen and Germans died. His secondary objective was the infliction of massive losses on the German army. Lt-Gen Sir Henry Rawlinson's Fourth Army in the centre shared a 25-mile front with Gen Edmund Allenby's Third Army further north. On Rawlinson's right the French Sixth Army would fight south of the river on an 11-mile front. A preliminary seven-day bombardment of the deep and well-prepared German defences consumed 1.7m shells in the longest artillery barrage to date. Attacking in waves against Maxims and much uncut wire despite the barrage, British and Commonwealth forces suffered nearly 60,000 casualties that first day, including 19,240 dead and 2,152 missing. It was the bloodiest in the British Army's history and the greatest loss by one side on any day of the war. By the mid-November finish the Allies had advanced barely 8 miles at a cost of 615,000 casualties (420,000 British), while German losses were upwards of 650,000. Falkenhayn had been forced to transfer units from Verdun, but at such cost.

The Somme battle produced fifty-one VCs, sixteen of them posthumously. It remains one of the most horrific examples of the impact of twentieth-century machine warfare on nineteenth-century infantry tactics.

Throughout the night before the battle opened on 1 July the slamming concussion of the barrage caused the war diary of the 14th Battalion Royal Irish Rifles to note: 'Heavy bombardment, great trouble in keeping the candle alight.' The Battalion was in crowded assembly trenches in Thiepval Wood, now a treeless waste. Six-foot Pte Billy McFadzean from Lurgan, County Armagh, was exchanging shouted banter above the thunder as Mills bombs were being distributed. At about 01.00 he grabbed a heavy box of twelve. It overturned, spilling grenades into the bottom of the trench and dislodging the pins in two of them. McFadzean unhesitatingly threw himself flat across them. He was blown to pieces, saving many lives. Apart from Pte Gillespie, who lost a leg, no one else was injured. It may be that rope securing the boxes had been ready cut to speed distribution and McFadzean failed to realise this. His VC was the first of ten to be won in France that day.

Sgt James Turnbull waited that same night with the 17th Battalion, Highland Light Infantry. The leading companies left their trenches just before 07.30 under a creeping barrage, getting to within 30–40yd of the German wire. When the barrage lifted, Sgt Turnbull and his men rushed a position of great importance to the enemy. Finding themselves unsupported on both flanks, however, they prepared a defence. Turnbull held the post the whole day against repeated and severe counter-attacks. On several occasions he maintained the position with great valour and skill almost single-handed when his party was nearly wiped out, before replacements could be brought up. Later in the day he was killed while bombing a counter-attack from the parados of a trench. He lies with his comrades in the Lonsdale cemetery nearby, at Authuile. His father and sister received his Cross from King George V.

Four sets of brothers have secured the VC. Roland and George Bradford were the last, and the only two who both won the Cross in the First World War. T/Lt-Col Roland Boys Bradford of the Durham Light Infantry (DLI) gained his during the Somme Battle. Lt-Cdr George Nicholson Bradford RN was awarded a posthumous VC after the Zeebrugge Raid in April 1918 (see pp. 125–6). The inspiring story of the 'Fighting Bradfords' includes their brothers, both with the DLI.

2/Lt James Bradford received the MC and Capt Thomas Bradford, the eldest, the DSO. Only Thomas survived the war.

Roland Bradford had landed in France as a second lieutenant with the 2nd Battalion in September 1914. Days later at Troyon he became the only surviving officer of his company. He received the MC the following February 'for services rendered in connection with operations in the field', at which time he was almost the only original officer of the Battalion to have escaped death or wounds. In August 1916 Bradford, aged 24 and now a lieutenant, was appointed T/Lt-Col and given command of the 9th Battalion, a Territorial Army unit from Gateshead. He turned it into one of the finest battalions in the British Army. It formed part of the 151st Brigade of 50th Division, which was ordered to capture Eaucourt l'Abbaye and trenches east of Le Sars on 1 October. The assault at 15.15 would be led by 6 DLI on the extreme right with Bradford's 9th close behind in support. The waiting Durhams were subjected to heavy German artillery and machine-gun fire as they crouched in trenches, the 6th suffering particularly badly. When its commanding officer was severely wounded, Bradford was ordered to lead the 6th as well as his own. The British barrage lifted and the 6th went over the top, its right flank exposed and unprotected by a division still struggling to reach position. They were raked with machine-gun fire at 550 rounds per minute from the enemy's uprated 08/15s. Bradford arrived as the attack stalled. His VC citation completes the story. 'By his fearless energy . . . and skilful leadership of the two battalions, regardless of all danger, he succeeded in rallying the attack, captured and defended the objective, and so secured the flank.' Bradford became a temporary brigadier-general and was given command of the 186th Brigade on 10 November 1917. Less than three weeks later, on the 30th, he was killed by a stray shell near his headquarters during the Battle of Cambrai.

Bradford was a charismatic leader of men with extraordinary powers of command. His battalion would do anything for him because they knew he was one among them, cared about them and asked nothing of them that he would not do himself. Tough men from the Durham coalfield knew a leader when they saw one. Bradford welcomed fresh replacements to the 9th Battalion with a stirring address delivered quietly and ending:

> The Call of Duty is a sacred one. We must do our duty, not merely to gain praise and advancement thereby, but because it is our duty, our duty to ourselves, our comrades, our Battalion, our families, our country, our King, and to the God who made us, and will help us in our work. You will find that you will be happy in this Battalion; you will find some splendid friends; your officers and non-commissioned officers are men who realise that they are made of the same sort of clay as you, and are in sympathy with your difficulties, and will do all they can to look after your interests. They know their job and will lead you well at all times. We are all working for the same purpose, the complete defeat of the enemy, and we must work together, each for each, and all for each. Upon behalf of the gallant lads whom I have had the honour to command, I welcome you to our midst. You are now of us, and will work with us and for us.
>
> My friends, I am going to arrange for the band to play one verse of the hymn 'Abide with me' every evening. I would like all of you then reverently to join in the words. It should mean more to you and me than the singing of a well-known hymn. 'Abide with me' should be no mere catch-phrase with us. It means that we realise that there is Someone who really abides with us, and who will help us to help ourselves. . . . He is with us, I say, just as our friends, Sergeant Caldwell, Corporal Guy, and Private Halley [all lately killed] are now serving with Him.

That fine hymn was adopted by the Battalion, then the Regiment, and remains the hymn of the Durham Light Infantry.

Roland Bradford at 25 was the youngest general in the British Army and one of its bravest and most respected new commanders. His gallant leadership was matched by an inspiring nobility of character. The Bradford family had no tradition of military service. George Bradford the father was a mining engineer and colliery owner of Milbanke, Darlington. Mrs Amy Bradford proudly wore the medals of her three dead sons at annual Armistice Day services, each of them an honour embracing the whole family.

'Q' Ships, February 1917

Cdr Gordon Campbell RN

To counter the U-boat menace a number of nondescript tramp steamers were converted into heavily armed sub-killers while retaining every appearance of ancient rust buckets. Their guns and depth charges were cunningly concealed, and crews were dressed and behaved as merchant seamen in a deadly game of bluff. The aim was to persuade U-boats to surface with the intention of sinking them by gunfire. Cdr Gordon Campbell became king of these 'Q' ships with his uncanny ability to find, deceive and destroy submarines. It nearly failed him, however, when HMS Q5 alias the *Farnborough* was torpedoed in the Irish Sea on 17 February 1917. Far from abandoning ship, all unwanted crew displayed a commendably rehearsed panic in taking to the boats and pulling furiously away while Campbell, his hidden gunners, and the men in the flooding engine compartment waited for U.83 either to surface or to finish *Farnborough* with another torpedo. After twenty agonising minutes it surfaced 300yd off. Campbell's first shot from a 6pdr hit the conning tower, killing its captain. The submarine was raked with fire until it rolled over and sank. Only two survivors were recovered. Campbell wryly signalled his vice-admiral: 'Q5 slowly sinking. Respectfully wishes you goodbye.' Escorts arrived and she was beached the following day.

Gordon Campbell sank three U-boats. His VC effectively embraced the entire crew. His deceptions included dressing a rating in fetching female attire and sitting him prominently in a deckchair on the poop. A member of the 'panic' party went so far as to make a dummy caged parrot to carry ostentatiously into the boat when 'abandoning ship'. Gordon Campbell left the Service as a vice admiral and became MP for Burnley.

The Merchant Navy

Master Archibald Bisset Smith

Capt Smith's indomitable act of defiance as commander of the cargo ship SS *Otaki* occurred on 10 March 1917. The merchantman's sole armament was a 4.7in gun for defensive purposes. She was sighted that afternoon by the disguised German raider *Moewe* mounting four 5.9in, one 4.1in and two 22pdr guns and two torpedo tubes. When Capt Smith refused to stop, a duel ensued for twenty minutes at ranges of 1,900–2,000yd. The *Otaki* scored several direct hits, causing considerable damage and starting a fire that lasted three days, but she herself was soon in sinking condition and heavily on fire, with casualties. Capt Smith ordered his crew away in boats, to be rescued. He went down with his ship, her colours flying. An enemy account considered it 'a duel as gallant as naval history can relate'. Capt Smith was awarded a posthumous VC.

Third Ypres, 31 July–10 November 1917

A/Capt Clement Robertson. Capt Noel Chavasse

After the disastrous Somme battles of 1916, FM Sir Douglas Haig persuaded the French to support a decisive British offensive in Flanders the following year. He planned to strike the German right flank, open a coastal corridor to the Dutch frontier and neutralise enemy submarine bases in Belgian ports. The Third Battle of Ypres opened on 31 July 1917 after a numbing fifteen-day bombardment from over 3,000 guns along 11 miles of front. It obliterated all water courses and land drainage. The assault, which was supported by 136 tanks, coincided with the onset of constant rain, creating a quagmire. The offensive finally submerged 4 miles on in the swamp wilderness of Passchendaele on 10 November. British and Commonwealth losses were 80,000 killed or missing, 230,000 wounded and 14,000 captured.

Capt Clement Robertson secured the first Tanks VC, yet he never fired a shot. He was not even inside a tank, but his act was considered one of the most stoically courageous of the war. The newly created Tank Corps was praying for a chance to prove itself and its revolutionary weapon in a massed surprise attack over good ground. Instead, Haig had consistently scattered his tanks in penny packets in minor infantry-support roles. Now they were sinking in the Flanders morass, perhaps taking the future of the Corps with them.

Robertson, a Section Commander in 3 Company, 1st Tank Battalion, and his batman Pte Allen worked almost continuously from 30 September to 3 October, frequently under fire, reconnoitring routes to get his Mk IVs to their lying-up positions and then to the start line. The two men also conducted hazardous surveys for the onward drive to enemy strongpoints at Reutel. Robertson knew the appalling conditions could lose him many machines if even one drifted slightly off line and sank its 28 tons in deep liquid mud. The backed-up column behind would be immobilised, unable to leave the track and unable to support the infantry at dawn. It would be blown to shrapnel when spotted. During the final move-up on the night of the 3rd he walked ahead of the lead machine, guiding the crawling column through a moonless night. It was usual to cup a lit cigarette behind one's back as a tail light, not least to avoid being accidentally run down if one stumbled.

Next morning at zero hour, 06.00, Robertson led the tanks on into battle at 3mph, still walking ahead despite increasingly heavy fire, and probing the saturated ground with his ashplant stick. They followed him across the Reutelbeek stream and onto a nominal 'road', which had just been pulverised for 500yd by the supporting artillery. Robertson could have boarded his tank but still he walked on, determined to see the section past this last obstacle. As the lead tank neared firmer ground, he fell, shot through the head, his mission most bravely accomplished. Capt Robertson was awarded a posthumous VC. Pte Allen received a well-earned DCM. The Reutel positions were taken. Weeks later the Corps finally had its chance, triumphantly proving the tanks at Cambrai on 20 November.

Of the three men who won Bars to their VCs, two were members of the Royal Army Medical Corps. Lt Arthur Martin-Leake was followed by Capt Noel Godfrey Chavasse, who gained his Bar at Third Ypres. Such men were giants. Noel Chavasse was born in 1884, his father becoming Bishop of Liverpool six years later. He took a first in Natural Sciences at Oxford, where he and his twin brother Christopher gained running Blues. Noel ran for England in the London Olympics of 1908. Christopher entered the Church of England. Noel studied medicine before joining the RAMC in 1913 on attachment to the 10th Battalion the Liverpool Scottish, of the King's (Liverpool) Regt. It landed in France on 3 November 1914. Christopher was already over there as chaplain to an Army hospital. It was he who would give Lt William Rhodes-Moorhouse VC his last Holy Communion as he lay dying at Merville in April 1915.

Noel Chavasse did much to ease the men's hardships in the trenches, where tetanus and trench foot were major concerns. Promoted Captain and Senior Medical Officer of the Brigade in August 1915, he wrote home: 'There is no glory attached to it. Existence is the only qualification.' His later outspoken criticism of the RAMC and of the lack of understanding and treatment of battle trauma were enough to stall further promotion. His bravery in tending and recovering the wounded under fire brought Chavasse the MC after the Hooge battle in June 1915, which practically destroyed the Liverpool Scottish. His continuing survival under fire in the Ypres salient became legendary. The battalion was recovered enough by September to join an attack on Sanctuary Wood nearby. Chavasse became a combatant, leaving his men and forming an ad hoc working party under fire to gather abandoned boxes of grenades, desperately needed by bombers holding a captured trench.

His first VC was gained at Guillemont on the Somme on 9 August 1916. During the attack Chavasse cared for many wounded lying in the open, working all day and through that night beneath heavy and unremitting fire. Next day he took a stretcher-bearer to bring an urgent case down from forward trenches. While carrying him back 500yd in murderous shellfire Chavasse received a splinter in the thigh. His first reaction on hearing of his recommendation for the Cross was to say that it would be worth having if it gave him a bit of extra home leave. His Bar to the VC followed in 1917 on the opening day of Third Ypres. It was one of fourteen Crosses gained on 31 July. Chavasse had set up his regimental aid post in a captured dugout, which was under bombardment. A splinter struck his head, possibly fracturing his skull, as he stood waving to indicate his location. Refusing to go to the rear for treatment after the wound was dressed, he returned to his duties at the aid post, where he was hit again at least once next day. Although practically without food, worn with fatigue and faint from his wounds, Chavasse worked on, searching at intervals for the injured lying out under fire. He saved many lives but was mortally wounded when a shell exploded in the post at 03.00 on 2 August. Hit in the stomach, he was taken to a Casualty Clearing Station at Brandhoeck. On the way he passed through the 46th Field Ambulance, whose CO at that time was Arthur Martin-Leake RAMC, VC and Bar.

Capt Noel Chavasse died on 4 August. The battalion's survivors, smothered in mud and near collapse from exhaustion, paraded for his funeral. Of the many tributes paid to him by his

King and senior commanders, the parade of his comrades remains the most poignant and fitting.

One Man's Air War, 1917/18

2/Lt Alan McLeod RFC

Flt Sub Lt Warneford, Lt Leefe Robinson, Capt 'Billy' Bishop, Capt Albert Ball, Capt James McCudden and Maj Edward Mannock are among the great air ace VCs whose stories are legendary. There were others whose exploits are less well known but whose guts and fine airmanship rank beside the best. One such was 2/Lt Alan Arnett 'Babe' McLeod VC, a Canadian from Stonewall, Winnipeg. Days after turning 18 and desperate to get into the war, he joined the Flying Corps in April 1917 and flew solo in less than three hours. Reaching England in August and praying for a scout squadron, he eventually got to France in December and was assigned to bombers with 2 Squadron, an Army cooperation unit flying slow Armstrong Whitworth FK8 twin-seat types. Undismayed, McLeod optimistically assumed a fighter role. He attacked a formation of eight vastly superior German Albatros scouts one day, enabling his bemused observer-gunner to shoot one down. Further successes included the destruction of an observation balloon, a dangerously explosive target even for faster aircraft, which had to get in close, shoot and break off at speed to avoid the resulting fireball and anti-aircraft guns defending the balloon site. Having narrowly achieved this, McLeod was attacked by three Albatros. Lt Reggie Key, his observer, put a well-directed burst of Lewis fire into the upper wing section of one that tried to get under their tail, the scout disintegrating as it fell in a steep dive. They fought their way out and got back unscathed.

The burly baby-faced Canadian won his VC on 27 March 1918, six days after Gen Ludendorff's dramatic spring offensive punched through a 60-mile section of the British front from Arras, south across the Somme to La Fère. Alan McLeod and

Lt A.W. Hammond MC, his observer, flew with six other FK8s on a bombing sortie to hit a troop concentration near Bray-sur-Somme. Poor visibility eventually broke up the formation. Pressing on alone, McLeod diverted after failing to find the target. Having spotted an appealing observation balloon, he had begun his dive when Hammond alerted him to a guardian Fokker triplane overhead. McLeod pulled out and climbed, enabling Hammond to squirt the Lewis and send the Fokker into an irrecoverable spin. A cab rank of eight more materialised, preparing to rake the FK8 in turn. As the first flew at them with flickering Spandaus Hammond coolly paused before putting a burst through the Fokker, which caught fire, the most terrifying and almost invariably terminal experience of many fliers in those days before parachutes.

The second triplane approached from below, its fire twice wounding Hammond, while a third machine making a simultaneous beam attack hit him again and sent a round through McLeod's leg. Hammond replied through waves of pain and nausea, his shots exploding the Fokker's fuel tank. The second machine returned, raking the FK8 from nose to tail, hitting McLeod in four places and rupturing fuel lines. The resultant fire quickly spread to the floors of both cockpits and the instrument panel. With his boots and the skirt of his flying coat on fire, McLeod hauled himself into the slipstream and on to the portside lower wing root. From there he leant into the now blazing cockpit, sideslipping the aircraft crabwise to deflect the trailing flames from Hammond, who had somehow got out and was lying on top of the fuselage, gripping his gun's Scarff traversing ring. Judging the bomber doomed, five of the remaining Fokkers withdrew. Incredibly, as the sixth circled to observe its downfall, Hammond managed to bring his gun to bear and shoot it down.

From this point on, any official recognition of their indomitable courage should have been posthumous. The weakened McLeod kept his footing against the slipstream blast.

In a feat of supreme airmanship he sufficiently controlled the plane to crash-land it between the lines, leaping clear as it hit the ground. Hammond was unconscious and still inside the burning wreck. Knowing its bomb load would go up at any moment, McLeod dragged himself aboard regardless of heavy machine-gun fire, freed his observer and carried him on his back for the agonising journey to the Allied trenches. When a shell splinter struck him he was forced to crawl, dragging Hammond to a shell-hole before collapsing from shock and loss of blood. Back in London his life hung in the balance before he was able to hobble to the Palace on two sticks to receive his VC from King George V. McLeod was still 18, the youngest recipient of an air VC of that war. He returned home to Stonewall to convalesce, only to die there on 9 November, a victim of the Spanish 'flu pandemic. The Armistice followed two days later. The brave Hammond lost his leg. He was awarded a Bar to his MC and later emigrated to Canada, settling in Winnipeg where McLeod lies buried.

Zeebrugge, 22–23 April 1918

Lt-Cdr George Bradford RN

Nearly a million tons of Allied merchant shipping were lost to German submarines in one month, April 1917, most of it British. Though opposed by the Admiralty, the convoy system was introduced under pressure from its younger commanders. This and other counter-measures had subdued but not broken the U-boat menace a year later, when the Navy audaciously sought to deny them access to their major base at Bruges. It was reached by canal from the ports at Ostend and Zeebrugge. If only the two canals could be blocked. Vice-Admiral Sir Roger Keyes planned simultaneous assaults on the two ports on St George's Day, 23 April 1918. The Ostend operation failed. At Zeebrugge three old minelayers laden with cement were sunk, but U-boat operations were only temporarily dislocated.

However, the propaganda value of the action was immense at a very dark period on the Western Front where Gen Ludendorff's break-through was threatening Amiens. Zeebrugge was stormed by nearly 2,000 men of the Royal Navy and Royal Marines on 22–23 April. The operation was conducted with vast courage. As a single action it secured eight VCs, second only to the eleven earned at Rorke's Drift. It is now virtually forgotten.

The squadron for Zeebrugge arrived at 23.40 on the 22nd. Storming parties from three ships were to mount a diversionary attack on the mile and a half long mole, disabling or distracting its heavy guns to ensure the three blockships passed safely to their scuttle positions at the canal mouth. Lt-Cdr George Nicholson Bradford RN, brother of Roland Bradford VC, commanded the Royal Marine party aboard *Iris II*, a requisitioned ferry. Speed was essential. A ferocious storm of hostile fire swept the mole, killing many among the assault groups waiting on open decks to disembark. A heavy swell prevented *Iris II* from securing alongside the mole. Realising his men's inability to land could prejudice the entire operation, Bradford climbed the ship's derrick carrying a ready-rigged parapet anchor, and perilously swung out over the side. It was not his task to make fast, but as the rise and fall of the ship dashed the derrick against the mole he waited his opportunity to jump, knowing he was close to death. He leaped, hooked-on the anchor, and seconds later fell between ship and mole riddled with bullets. His body was never recovered. On this, his thirty-first birthday, George Bradford joined brother Roland in valiant death, both honoured with the Victoria Cross.

The Unknown Warriors

The United States awarded the Congressional Medal of Honor to the British Unknown Warrior in March 1921. It was in this spirit that Britain reciprocated, awarding and engraving a Victoria Cross to 'The Unknown Warrior of the United States of

America'. It was presented by Admiral of the Fleet Earl Beatty on Armistice Day, 11 November 1921, at Arlington National Cemetery. A card signed by King George V was attached to the wreath: 'As unknown, and yet well known; As dying, and, behold we live.'

The possibility of a similar award to the French Unknown Warrior was considered in London in 1921, and again three years later at the request of 'The Friends of France', of which FM Earl Haig was president. The War Office feared this would precipitate a mass exchange between the Allies, and, having already put the Italians off, it could hardly now favour France. The War Office informed 'The Friends' in August 1924 that 'It would be unwise to take the action which you suggest'.

*   *   *

There remained one for whom release from a war of unspeakable sacrifice stirred unfathomable emotions. In a letter to *The Times*, 28 April 1919, E.H. Swan of 45A Linden Gardens W2 wrote:

Sir, can you do something to stop the threatened peace celebrations? The best classes have lost so many they love and so much of their wealth that they are sure to be out of everything, and that leaves it in the hands of our present shopping and cinema class, which surely has had benefit enough from the war.

7

Bolshevists and Bushfires, 1919–1938

The arm of the government is long . . .
its officers fly like birds.

(From leaflets dropped by the RAF
over Iraqi villages, 1930s)

Of the ten VCs awarded for actions between January 1919 and December 1938, five were gained in north Russia, four on India's north-west frontier and one in the Middle East. In all, five Crosses were awarded posthumously.

RUSSIA, KRONSTADT, 1919

Lt Augustine Agar RN. Cdr Claude Dobson RN. Lt Gordon Steele RN

Russia's withdrawal from the war following the revolution in November 1917 precipitated a confused and undeclared Allied war of intervention with Bolshevik Russia. A force with strong British support was dispatched in March 1918, ostensibly to protect Allied military equipment stockpiled in Russia's northern ports. Its covert task was to train Tsarist White Russian troops in support of a new eastern front. The force had to over-winter there. To secure its evacuation Britain sent a North Russia Relief Force which arrived in June 1919. Its first concern was the enemy's powerful Baltic fleet at Kronstadt in the heavily defended Gulf of Finland.

Lt Augustine Agar commanded HM Coastal Motor Boat 4, one of a flotilla of new high-speed ultra shallow-draught torpedo craft ideal for striking enemy shipping in mined waters. He led an attack on the fleet at Kronstadt on the night of 16–17 June. They penetrated a destroyer screen and were closing with the Russian cruiser *Oleg* when CMB4's torpedo launch cartridge misfired, halting the boat for 20 minutes for noisy repairs. The Russians heard nothing before Agar resumed the attack and sank the 7,000-ton cruiser. Again evading the destroyers, they safely recrossed the Gulf to their Finnish base at Terrioki. King George V spent half an hour in discussion with Lt Agar when investing him with the VC for this action, and presenting the DSO for Agar's part in a successful return to Kronstadt on 18 August.

The repeat attack on the night of 18 August was a combined operation. While aircraft from *Vindictive* made diversionary attacks, Cdr Claude Dobson in CMB31 led motor boats into Kronstadt's harbour through very heavy machine-gun fire where he torpedoed the battleship *Petropavlosk*. As CMB88 entered, its commanding officer Lt Dayrell-Read was shot through the head, and the craft was thrown off course. Lt Gordon Steele took the wheel and steadied her, lifted Dayrell-Read clear and torpedoed the battleship *Andrei Pervozanni* only 100yd distant. A very tight turn followed to get a view of *Petropavlosk* through the smoke before Steele torpedoed her again. Both ships were sunk. The fort and batteries guarding the harbour on their way out were exuberantly raked with fire from every machine gun aboard. Cdr Dobson and Lt Steele won Crosses for the operation, which also sank a submarine depot ship. Lt Agar had led in a column of CMBs before falling back to divert the harbour defences.

INDIA, NORTH-WEST FRONTIER, 1919–1935

Lt William Kenny

Mahsud tribesmen along the volatile north-west frontier of India began attacking British-occupied towns and military installations in May 1919. The insurrection was met with a force of 63,000 men of the Indian Army. On 2 January 1920 Lt William David Kenny of 4/39th Garhwal Rifles commanded a company in an advanced covering position near Kot Kai. They held it for more than four hours, repulsing three determined attacks by greatly superior numbers of rebels. Kenny, an Irishman from Dundalk, was foremost in the hand-to-hand fighting and repeatedly responded with bomb and bayonet. Their brave stand protected the flank on which the success of operations depended. When the subsequent withdrawal was slowed by the wounded, Kenny turned back with a handful of his men and counter-attacked, all knowing they must die and praying they would not be left wounded before a merciless enemy. They fought to the last. Kenny was honoured with a posthumous VC.

VCs were also gained in this region by T/Capt Henry Andrews, Indian Medical Service, on 22 October 1919; Sepoy Ishar Singh, 28th Punjab Regiment, on 10 April 1921, the first Sikh soldier to be awarded the Cross; and Capt Godfrey Meynell, 5th Battalion Corps of Guides, 12 Frontier Force Regiment, Indian Army, near Mohmand on 29 September 1935. Only Ishar Singh survived.

ARAB REVOLT, MESOPOTAMIA, 1920

Capt George Henderson

After the First World War the Middle Eastern territories of the German and Ottoman empires were divided by the League of Nations and assigned to the victors, who were mandated to guide them to eventual self-government. Britain became responsible for Mesopotamia (Iraq) and Palestine. In Iraq, Sunni and Shia Muslim clerics joined to foment a rebellion that the war-weary British sought to quell largely from the air with punitive bombing raids.

Capt George Henderson MC DSO, 2nd Battalion the Manchester Regiment, was 15 miles from Hillah, Mesopotamia, on the evening of 24 July 1920 when he was ordered to retire with his company. After 500yd a large party of Arabs opened fire from the flank, causing his men to split up and waver. Regardless of the danger, Henderson immediately reorganised the company and led it in a bayonet charge, driving off the enemy. He later led two further charges, during the second of which he fell wounded. Refusing to leave his command, he was hit again on reaching the enemy. He knew that he was mortally wounded, and asked an NCO to hold him up, murmuring: 'I'm done now, don't let them beat you.' A posthumous VC saluted Capt George Henderson's fine leadership and courageous example.

8

The Second World War, 1939–1945

Now I shall have to go and earn it.
*(Flt Lt James Brindley Nicolson VC
on receiving his award, 1940)*

Nazi Germany's programme of territorial expansion by coercion
and force began with the murder of Austria's Chancellor (1934),
the return of the Saar to Germany (1935), the remilitarisation of
the Rhineland (1936), the annexation of Austria and of the
Sudetenland area of Czechoslovakia (1938), followed in 1939
by the annexation of Bohemia and Moravia and Germany's
invasion of Poland on 1 September. The whole ghastly
progression was met for the most part with diplomatic hand-
wringing in the Chancelleries of Europe. With the rape of
Poland, Franco-British guarantees of Polish sovereignty
compelled action. On 3 September a shocked Prime Minister
Neville Chamberlain informed the nation that it was now at war
with Germany. Gen Lord Gort VC led a British Expeditionary
Force to France. By March 1940 it totalled eight divisions,
nearly a quarter of a million men. The 'phoney war' on the
Western Front ended in May with Germany's invasion of the
Low Countries and France. Evacuation of 338,000 British,
French and other Allied troops from Dunkirk followed in May
and June. When France fell on 25 June, Britain stood alone and
almost defenceless, bracing for invasion. If the Germans could
break the Royal Air Force they would assuredly remove all hope
for occupied Europe.

The war brought 182 awards of the Victoria Cross, including one Bar. Of these, some ninety were posthumously awarded.

Invasion of Denmark and Norway, April 1940

Lt-Cdr Gerard Roope RN. Capt Bernard Warburton-Lee RN

Germany invaded Denmark and Norway on 9 April 1940, supported by the battlecruisers *Scharnhorst* and *Gneisenau* and the heavy cruiser *Admiral Hipper*. Lt-Cdr Gerard Broadmead Roope, commanding HM destroyer *Glowworm*, engaged two enemy destroyers on the 8th, while heading alone to Norway's West Fjord. She hit one, after which they broke off and moved north. Realising he was being drawn towards the enemy's battleships, Roope unhesitatingly gave chase. The 10,000-ton *Hipper* was duly sighted bearing down on *Glowworm*, 1,345 tons, in very heavy seas, which prevented Roope from shadowing it until HMS *Renown* could arrive. In a bravely defiant action he alerted the Home Fleet before turning to engage the cruiser. *Glowworm* fired ten torpedoes without result. When finally his gallant ship was crippled and burning he turned her, and with her three remaining guns blazing, rammed *Hipper*'s bow, tearing a hole that forced the cruiser's return to Germany for repairs. *Glowworm* fell back, resumed firing and scored a hit before heeling over and sinking. Of her complement of 119, only one officer and thirty men were saved and captured. Gerard Roope went down with his ship. He was honoured with the first VC of the war, though it was not gazetted until 1945, when the story became known.

The Cross was gained by Capt Bernard Warburton-Lee in HMS *Hardy* on the 10th when he was commanding a flotilla of five destroyers under orders to attack Narvik. The port contained six enemy destroyers and a submarine. Its approaches were believed to be mined. Warburton-Lee attacked in a snowstorm at dawn, leading his flotilla up the fjord and totally surprising the enemy. He first torpedoed a destroyer bearing the pennant of the Commodore, killing him, before sinking another and spraying gunfire over the remainder to such effect that they offered little resistance. Several German merchant ships were also sunk. Until then Warburton-Lee's destroyers had remained untouched, but five more German warships drew near and in the ensuing action he was killed when *Hardy*'s bridge took a direct hit. Another shell destroyed the engine room, and, still under fire, the crippled destroyer was beached. Warburton-Lee's last message to the flotilla was 'Continue to engage the enemy'.

Darkest Hours, 1940

2/Lt Richard Annand. Flt Lt James Brindley Nicolson. A/Capt E.S. Fogarty Fegen RN

Germany's blitzkrieg opened on 10 May. Panzer divisions supported by the Luftwaffe fought hard and drove fast across Holland, Belgium and France. By 25 June all three countries had been defeated and most of the British Expeditionary Force had been evacuated, losing all its guns, transport and heavy equipment.

In Belgium on 15 May a company of the 2nd Battalion Durham Light Infantry fought to delay the enemy repairing a blown road bridge over the River Dyle east of Brussels. The German assault began with mortar fire at dawn, hitting D Company's position near the bridge. Under heavy covering fire the enemy then moved a repair party into the sunken river bottom. 2/Lt Richard 'Dickie' Annand's platoon kept it pinned down until ammunition ran out. He called for grenades and ran alone across open ground under mortar and machine-gun fire to the bridge from where he drove out the party below, inflicting over twenty casualties and himself becoming wounded.

When the enemy launched another attack that evening Annand again went forward with grenades and inflicted more casualties. His sergeant remembers that feeding Annand's appetite for grenades was like giving strawberries to an elephant. The badly shot-up platoon was recalled at 23.00. Annand later learned that his batman Pte Joseph Hunter had been left behind, severely wounded and unable to walk. He returned to the position and, finding a wheelbarrow, he got Hunter into it before setting off back. Too weak to lift him over a fallen tree, however, he was eventually forced to leave him and seek help. Annand reached his old Company Headquarters to find it deserted. He pressed on, finally collapsing from exhaustion and loss of blood, when a Bren carrier crew found him. Hunter was captured and died of his wounds on 17 June. Richard Annand received the VC from King George VI at Buckingham Palace, accompanied by the sound of AA gunfire during an air raid. His was the first Cross of the war to be awarded to the Army.

The Battle of Britain was arguably the most critical in British history yet it secured just one VC. Of the thirty-two Crosses awarded to airmen during the Second World War, this alone went to Fighter Command. The 'damn your eyes' courage of Flt Lt 'Nick' Nicolson inspired the nation at a time of crisis. His cross was gained in the first air combat of the 23-year-old from Shoreham, Sussex.

Nicolson took off from Boscombe Down with 249 Squadron in Hurricane P3576 on a cloudless 16 August 1940. As they patrolled the Poole–Ringwood–Salisbury sector he spotted three Junkers 88 bombers 4 miles off and was cleared to break in pursuit, leading his section of three Hurricanes. The enemy encountered Spitfires, which shot all three down before he got there. Nicolson was climbing over Southampton when his cockpit exploded with flying metal and perspex fragments as cannon shells ripped into his aircraft. His section had been jumped by Messerschmitt Bf110s, which left Plt Off King's Hurricane in flames. He baled out, but an undisciplined anti-aircraft unit fired on him, destroying his parachute and sending him to his death. The second Hurricane was badly shot up and made a forced landing. Nicolson was in grave trouble. A shell had driven a shard of perspex into his left eye almost severing the lid, another ignited 28 gallons of fuel in the spare tank, while the third tore off his right trouser leg and a fourth struck his left heel.

Cursing himself for a fool as he took evasive action, and with blood blinding one eye, Nicolson saw a Messerschmitt shoot past beneath him and fully into his gunsight. Oblivious of his wounds and the fuel fire on the starboard side just forward of the cockpit, he remembered shouting 'I'll teach you some manners you . . . Hun'. Their dive touched 400 mph as Nicolson's eight Browning MGs raked the Messerschmitt. It was seen by observers to crash into the sea. He noticed almost dispassionately that his left hand was burning, the skin peeling as it gripped the throttle lever. Nicolson thrust upwards to bale out, forgetting to open the hood and striking his head on the smashed frame. It slid easily, but in his haste he had not released four restraining straps, which bounced him back into the blazing cockpit. Fumbling with badly damaged hands, he came free and fell clear, near-trouserless and with his shredded tunic smouldering. Nicolson had little difficulty feigning death as a Messerschmitt screamed by before turning for another pass. He could recall only that, if it fired, it missed him. His left knuckle was burned to the bone, the flesh of his other hand loosened, and he had facial burns above his oxygen mask. His shoe was spilling blood. Avoiding a sea landing, which in his condition would have drowned him, he was instead hit in the backside by a Local Defence Volunteers sergeant with a shotgun. He had been in the air for forty-seven minutes – and half a lifetime.

Nicolson fought for his life before making a slow recovery, going operational again a year later. He was conscious that others had done as much or more to deserve the Cross, and was determined to prove his own worthiness. He succeeded to the command of 27 Squadron in Burma, flying Mosquitos against ground targets and winning the DFC. He died in a Liberator on a bombing sortie, flying as 'observer', when a double engine fire caused it to crash into the Bay of Bengal on 2 May 1945. 'Nick' Nicolson's logbooks dryly refer to his dogfights as 'local amusement'. Circumstances compelled his widow to put his medals up for auction in 1983. The RAF Museum at Hendon was determined to secure them, as was an ex-RAF collector. The group with its VC was expected to fetch £25,000. The hammer fell at £105,000. It transpired that the collector was trying to get the medals in order to present them to the museum against which he had unknowingly bid. The nation's wholly inadequate war widow's pension had failed Mrs Nicolson. It took a bidder's oversight to assure her a secure old age.

The Battle of Britain ended in victory for the RAF with 1,733 claimed German aircraft destroyed and 915 British losses. The intensive bombing of England's cities began in earnest in November.

E.S. Fogarty Fegen captained HMS *Jervis Bay*, a poorly armed ex-liner packed with empty oil drums to aid buoyancy if torpedoed. She was sole escort to thirty-eight merchantmen in heavy Atlantic seas on 5 November 1940. Sighting the pocket battleship *Admiral Scheer*, Fegen made straight for it, laying a smokescreen and positioning his ship between the raider and her prey, enabling them to scatter. Outgunned and outranged, *Jervis Bay* quickly lost her steering, followed by her 6in guns. She distracted the *Scheer* and took its fire for nearly an hour, receiving salvo after salvo from 11in and 5.9in guns. When *Jervis Bay*'s flag was shot away, a man seen to climb the rigging and nail another to the mast. Capt Fegen, son of a Vice Admiral, was last sighted on the smashed bridge with an almost severed arm as his burning ship settled and went down. Sixty-five crew were saved that night by a Swedish merchant vessel that had stayed back. Skipper Sven Olander returned after mustering his crew and taking a vote. At least thirty-three precious ships of the convoy were saved. Fogarty Fegen's posthumous VC honoured a most gallant captain and his entire crew.

The Desert War, 1941–1942

Cpl John Edmondson. T/Lt-Col Henry Foote. Pte Adam Wakenshaw

Gen Sir Archibald Wavell, C-in-C Middle East, launched a successful westward drive in North Africa in December 1940 to destroy Italian forces in Cyrenaica. Tobruk on the North African coast was captured by Australian troops on 22 January 1941. Germany's Afrika Korps under Gen Erwin Rommel launched an effective counter-strike east along the coast towards the Suez Canal in March. Tobruk held out, becoming besieged on 13 April.

Cpl John 'Jack' Edmondson, 2/17th (New South Wales) Battalion, won Australia's first VC of the war on the night of 13/14 April. Thirty German infantry had broken through Tobruk's perimeter to clear the way for a tank assault. They opened a heavy fire on a key strongpoint 100yd away, held by a platoon under Lt Mackell with a section led by Cpl Edmondson. Under covering fire from the strongpoint Mackell, Edmondson and five men charged the enemy with fixed bayonets, hurling grenades. Edmondson was hit in the neck and stomach by machine-gun fire but kept going, killing at least two Germans, as reported by Mackell. Hearing Mackell's shout, Edmondson turned to see him standing with his bayonet pushed into a man who was gripping him about the legs while another was about to attack Mackell from behind. Though mortally wounded, Edmondson managed to save Mackell's life, killing both Germans with his bayonet and then another before collapsing. He died soon afterwards. The enemy position was cleared and its assault was wrecked next day by the Australians and the Royal Horse Artillery. Tobruk was bravely held for eight months until relieved in December.

Surprisingly, of the six VCs won by the men of the tanks in both world wars, five were gained while on foot. Lt-Col Henry 'Fairy' Foote was the possible exception, though he too spent much of his time dismounted. The short square-built regular officer commanded 7th Battalion Royal Tank Regiment. He had already won the DSO before the Afrika Korps resumed its drive on Tobruk in May 1942. Rommel launched his assault on the Gazala defence line 35 miles west of the port on the 27th. Foote's VC citation spans the full twenty days of the ensuing battle. It ended in a fighting withdrawal followed by the loss of Tobruk.

Foote led the 7th in a counter-attack with 42nd RTR on 6 June, characteristically riding outside his tank despite intense fire until the Matilda was knocked out. As he mounted another, an MG bullet tore the side of his neck. In pain and despite the danger, he refused to ride inside, remaining on the hull until that tank was also disabled. Foote then walked from crew to crew giving orders and encouragement, helping remove wounded and, by his imperturbable example, steadying and inspiring his men. When the commander of the 42nd was killed, Foote assumed control of both battalions, rallying them and pulling them back in good order. By dusk he had defeated the enemy's attempt to encircle two divisions. His force had lost sixty-four of its seventy-six tanks whose liability to catch fire, and poor gunsights and ammunition, were a greater weakness than their 2pdr main armament.

On 13 June the enemy attempted to surround the Guards Brigade on an escarpment. The Panzers had to be delayed so that the Guards could withdraw that night. Foote's supporting force was down to some twenty-five Matildas. His command tank was hit early on in a storm of fire. Approaching exhaustion and suffering from his wound, he dismounted and again directed his men on foot, knowing he had to hold the flank until well after dark. A violent three-hour sandstorm intervened, after which the tanks were subjected to saturation shelling with HE and 88mm fire which incinerated the lead squadron. Foote drove ahead standing upright in his turret and signalling 'Conform to my movements'. Flanked by the two remaining squadrons and supported by the excellent new 6pdr anti-tank guns, the tanks advanced through smoke and engaged the enemy. No sooner had the Germans found their range than Foote pulled back under smoke before repeatedly advancing and retiring to confuse the enemy and reduce the heavy punishment his force was taking. Though his own tank's guns were disabled he continued to direct the crews until the enemy fell silent in approaching darkness. Seven Matildas were lost, but the corridor was kept open and the brigade marched through.

'Fairy' Foote's high courage, inspired leadership and tactical skills were justly rewarded with the Cross. He was captured a week later after breaking his leg while trying to escape from an encircled Tobruk. During captivity in Italy he escaped and joined the partisans before reaching neutral Switzerland – where he found the skiing excellent. He was later appointed Major-General and became Director, Royal Armoured Corps.

Tobruk fell to Rommel in hard fighting on 21 June. Before dawn on the 27th his troops encountered the 151st Brigade south of Mersa Matruh. On a rocky plateau the 9th Battalion Durham Light Infantry had hastily constructed low piles of stone in lieu of foxholes. Four anti-tank guns were positioned ahead on a forward slope, one per company. Pte Adam Wakenshaw, aged 28, a very tough Geordie from the Durham coalfields, was among the crews. As the enemy advanced under a full moon, his 2pdr put a round through the engine of a tractor hauling a light gun at 200yd. A following gun opened up, and Wakenshaw's position came under intense mortar and shell fire, killing or wounding all its gunners.

Wakenshaw lay with his left arm blown off above the elbow. Seeing the enemy attempting to reach their own stranded gun, he crawled back to his 2pdr, where Pte Eric Mohn its aimer was also badly wounded. With Wakenshaw as one-armed loader they got off five rounds, a direct hit damaging the light gun and burning its tractor. An incoming shell then killed Mohn and further injured Wakenshaw, who was blown some distance.

Unbelievably, he dragged himself back yet again, cradled another round into the breech and was about to fire when a direct hit on the ammunition killed him instantly and wrecked the gun. The three forward rifle companies, which had helplessly watched the drama ahead of them, were progressively overrun and captured. When the enemy withdrew that night, Wakenshaw was buried beside his shattered gun. It now rests in Durham's DLI Museum, an enduring witness of his act of supreme valour, which Ptes Eric Mohn and Pat Murray, its other crewmen, also bravely showed. Pte Adam Wakenshaw was honoured with a posthumous VC.

'In the presence of the enemy'

Lt Peter Roberts RN. PO Thomas Gould RN
Chaplain Sqn Ldr The Revd Herbert Pugh GC RAFVR

Since 1881 the VC Warrant has confined award of the Cross to acts of most conspicuous bravery, valour or self-sacrifice 'in the presence of the enemy', while the George Cross of equal merit, instituted in 1940, honours members of the armed forces and civilians for such acts not in the enemy's presence. But determining just how 'present' the enemy must be for award of the VC or the GC has created puzzling anomalies.

HM submarine *Thrasher* sank a heavily escorted supply ship in the Mediterranean off Crete on 16 February 1942. She was immediately subjected to a three-hour depth-charge attack and aerial bombing. When Capt Mackenzie surfaced at nightfall, the sub's motion revealed the presence of two unexploded bombs. They had failed to detonate only because she had been diving and must have reached periscope depth when they hit. The first bomb was rolling about on deck and was jettisoned. The other presented a real and highly dangerous problem. It had penetrated the side plating of the gun emplacement and then the lightweight deck casing above the pressure hull, on which the bomb now lay.

Lt Peter Roberts and PO Tommy 'Nat' Gould volunteered to enter the confined space, no more than 2ft high in places between hull and deck casing, to manhandle the bomb 20ft in pitch darkness to the nearest hinged deck grating. Lying flat, they wormed past iron deck supports, battery ventilators and drop bollards. Gould then rolled onto his back, cradling the heavy 100lb bomb across his stomach. Roberts lay behind him face down, head to head, hauling and guiding Gould backwards by his shoulders. Each time the explosively unstable bomb moved, it emitted an unnerving 'twang', like a broken spring. Meantime *Thrasher* was surfaced, stationary, close inshore in enemy waters and still being hunted. Roberts and Gould knew they would drown if she had to crash-dive. It took them forty agonising minutes before the bomb was hoisted on deck, wrapped in sacking and lowered carefully over the bow.

Sir Andrew Cunningham, C-in-C Mediterranean, recommended both men for the VC. The Honours and Awards Committee in London disagreed, arguing that the acts of bravery did not occur in the presence of the enemy and therefore the George Cross was appropriate. Cunningham pointed out they were removing enemy bombs within sight of an enemy coastline and that should be good enough for anybody. Peter Roberts and Tommy Gould received well-deserved Crosses for saving their comrades and the vessel. Both men survived the war. It was all a far cry from the seconds-long action of Mate Charles Lucas of *Hecla* and the first VC, eighty-eight years previously.

Sqn Ldr The Revd Herbert Cecil Pugh RAFVR performed surely one of the most quietly inspiring acts of heroism of the war. He was aboard HM Troopship *Anselm* bound for West Africa with 1,300 servicemen when she was torpedoed in the Atlantic on 5 July 1941. A hold below the waterline was severely damaged, trapping airmen and destroying their means of escape. Herbert Pugh insisted on being lowered into the wrecked and flooding space from a hatch, though the ship was foundering and the weather deck was awash. He simply explained that he must go where his men were. He was lowered on a rope to try to reach and comfort them. Minutes later, attempts were made to haul up the padre as the ship listed before sinking. The rope had gone slack. He had untied himself, and went down with the trapped airmen. Chaplain Sqn Ldr Pugh's decision sprang from deep spiritual conviction and a profound sense of duty. He was awarded a posthumous George Cross.

It may be thought the parallels with *Thrasher* are such that Herbert Pugh should have received the VC for his devoted self-sacrifice. The U-boat that torpedoed *Anselm* with the loss of 254 lives was doubtless a very present enemy, typically standing-off to observe and readied to fire a final torpedo if necessary.

Bomber Command, April 1942

Sqn Ldr John Nettleton RAF

Twelve Lancaster bombers took off for a flight deep into Southern Germany on 17 April 1942 on one of the most important precision raids of the war. The MAN (Maschinenfabrik Augsburg Nürnberg AG) factory at Augsburg produced half the diesel engines for Germany's U-boats, plus heavy tanks and engines for other AFVs. The newly introduced Lancasters were to go in broad daylight. Over 1,000 miles of the sortie would be above hostile territory. They must keep below 50ft to stay under German radar, and maintain that very exacting altitude in darkness on the long return. Bomb loads were reduced from 22,000lb to 4,000lb to economise fuel consumption. It was a near-suicidal proposition. Six aircraft were flown from each of 44 and 97 Squadrons. Sqn Ldr John Dering Nettleton from Natal commanded 44's section. He would earn South Africa's first VC of the war.

Soon after entering enemy airspace Nettleton's formation encountered some twenty-five fighters. His rear guns became disabled and four of his six Lancasters were shot down. The mission had barely begun. Flying at treetop height at up to

175 mph for most of an arduous five-hour flight to target, the remaining bombers encountered intense and accurate flak over Augsburg. The two aircraft made their bombing run together, so low that some flak batteries were firing into buildings. Nettleton and Flg Off J. Garwell, piloting the other Lanc, held course through exploding shells until at last the planes leapt on release of their four delayed-action bombs over the engine shops. Garwell's Lancaster was hit by flak, burst into flames and crash-landed. Amazingly, Nettleton got his home, riddled with holes, having evaded the hundreds of fighters scrambled across southern Germany to hunt down the survivors. Of eighty-five crew who flew out, forty-nine were missing. Much was made of the bomb damage at the time, but in fact it was disappointing. Captured German reports record seventeen direct hits, five of which were duds. This in no way detracts from the unflinching and professional performance of Nettleton and all the crews, many of whom gave their lives. Wg Cdr John Nettleton was killed over Turin on 13 July 1943.

The Last Double-VC

Capt Charles Upham

Capt Charles Hazlitt Upham was the third and last to become a double-VC. A stocky, pugnacious and hard-swearing 33-year-old from Christchurch, New Zealand, Upham was the son of a lawyer; war was to forge him into a truly outstanding soldier and junior leader. Significantly, the citations for both his VCs covered not one but many actions over days of sustained gallantry. He first gained the Cross as a Second Lieutenant with C Company, 20 Battalion, 2nd New Zealand Division, during the German invasion of Crete in May 1941. The Division was among the British and Empire troops evacuated there from Greece the previous month, many arriving in Crete with only the clothes they stood in. An *ad hoc* defence force of 30,000 men was formed, British, Australian, Kiwis and some Greeks, desperately short of weapons and equipment but full of fighting spirit. Crack German paratroop and glider-borne units invaded on 20 May in the most successful deployment of airborne forces of the war. Next day they seized the vital Maleme airfield. Two of Maj-Gen Bernard Freyberg's battalions, the 20th and the Kiwis, were ordered to counter-attack that night, the 21st.

For the next nine days and nights Charles Upham displayed outstanding leadership, courage and cunning in close-quarter fighting, for which his preferred weapon was invariably a sackful of grenades. Typically, he would run ahead lobbing grenades into a weapon pit or a building before calling his boys to mop up. Suffering severe dysentery, he was blown up by one mortar shell, badly wounded in the shoulder by another, and shot in the foot. Refusing hospitalisation he fought on, one arm in a sling. A fighting withdrawal was ordered on the 23rd. Upham sent his platoon back while remaining to warn others. Two approaching Germans saw him and came on firing Schmeissers. Upham tripped and fell. Crawling through scrub he reached an olive tree and rose slowly, resting his rifle in a fork. With difficulty he shot the first, knowing he must re-cock, aim and fire single-handed before the second had time to return fire. He managed it, the German falling so close that he brushed the muzzle. Charles Upham's contribution to the successful withdrawal was out of all proportion to the size of his force. His genuine modesty showed when, on receiving the VC, he declared that it was not down to bravery but to circumstance.

Upham was again suffering from dysentery throughout the nine days during which he gained the Bar. Now a company commander and still with 20 Battalion, he was engaged in operations in the Western Desert, culminating in the attack on El Ruweisat Ridge on the night of 14/15 July 1942. Despite being twice wounded, once when crossing fireswept ground to inspect his forward sections guarding minefields, and again when he completely destroyed with grenades a truckload of German troops, he insisted on remaining with his men for the final assault.

During the opening stages Upham's company was in reserve. When communications with the forward troops broke down, he was instructed to send up an officer to report progress. Upham grabbed a prized Spandau light automatic and went himself, returning with the information after several sharp encounters with enemy MG posts. His company was ordered forward just before dawn on the 15th. Nearing its objective, it met very heavy fire from four machine-gun positions and several tanks. Upham immediately led his men in an attack on the two nearest strongpoints, his shouted encouragement clearly audible above the gunfire. They overcame fierce resistance to take the emplacements. Although shot through the elbow and breaking his arm – his third wound – Upham had personally destroyed a tank and several guns and vehicles with grenades. He went on again to a forward position, returning with some of his men who had become isolated. He continued to dominate the situation until the company had beaten off a violent counter-attack and consolidated the position. Exhausted and weakened from loss of blood, Upham then consented to have his wounds dressed before returning to his men. There he stayed for the rest of the day under heavy shell fire until he was again severely wounded. Unable to move, he was taken prisoner when his gallant company was reduced to six survivors, and over-run. Upham's repeated escape attempts as a POW ended with detention at Colditz. His hatred of all things German never left him.

Upham's entitlement to the Bar or any lesser decoration was questioned at Middle East HQ. No recommendation reached London until mid-1945. The Army Council had ruled in 1917 that an award could be made to a POW provided the act for which he was recommended was unconnected with the circumstances in which he had been taken prisoner. This was condemned as lacking reality by Gen Ruggles-Brise the Military Secretary at GHQ France in 1918. These official misgivings carried over to the Second World War. When the Committee on the Grant of Honours, Decorations and Medals in Time of War met on 18 July 1940 it agreed that such awards could be made but should not be invited. Any submissions would simply receive consideration. It was Upham's divisional commander in 1942, Gen Freyberg VC, who sought to reopen the case in July 1945. Gen McCreery, commander of the Eighth Army, agreed with his predecessor Gen Alexander that a DSO was appropriate, and forwarded the papers to London for the first time for decision. Gen Wemyss, Military Secretary, supported award of the Bar, as did Gen Eisenhower, the Supreme Allied Commander. In approving the submission King George VI added that he would like to see Upham, but by then he had returned home to Christchurch to resume farming. Charles Upham's Bar was gazetted in September 1945. This outstanding soldier and one of New Zealand's finest sons died in November 1994.

The Seagrim Brothers

T/Lt-Col Derek Seagrim. T/Maj Hugh Seagrim GC

Brothers Derek Anthony and Hugh Paul Seagrim remain the only instance where the Victoria Cross and the George Cross were awarded to the same family. By March 1943 the Afrika Corps had been driven back 1,300 miles by Gen Bernard Montgomery's Eighth Army following its victory at Alamein the previous October. Rommel was recalled to Germany. His force had retreated behind the formidable defensive line of Mareth in Tunisia – an anti-tank ditch 12ft wide and 8ft deep, with concrete emplacements and minefields. Lt-Col Derek Seagrim, commanding 7 Battalion The Green Howards, gained his VC on 20/21 March in the opening night assault on the line. A murderous German artillery, mortar and machine-gun fire threatened to delay the battalion and thus the main attack. Realising the seriousness of the situation as casualties mounted, Seagrim placed himself at its head and rallied a confused company at the ditch, helping to place a scaling ladder across and being first over before personally assaulting two enemy machine-gun positions with pistol and grenades, killing or capturing twenty Germans. His gallant leadership brought capture of the position. The Battalion overcame a very determined counter-attack next morning, Seagrim directing fire and moving about imperturbably. The attackers were wiped out to a man. Derek Seagrim died two weeks later in the Battle of Akarit, not knowing he had won the VC.

Seagrim's elder brother Hugh, an Indian Army Major with 19 Battalion The Hyderabad Regiment, held the DSO and the MBE. He was attached to Force 136 in Burma and had led a covert party in the Keren Hills deep behind the lines since February 1943. The Japanese eventually began a widespread campaign of arrests and torture to discover his location. The following February they arrested 270 Kerens, torturing and killing many. Though the people continued to aid Seagrim, he surrendered himself on 15 March to spare them further suffering. He was taken to Rangoon with eight others, and all were sentenced to death. Hugh Seagrim pleaded that only he should be executed, as the others were merely acting on his orders. Such was their devotion to him that they all demanded to die with him. These quite exceptionally brave men were all executed on 22 September in Rangoon. Hugh Seagrim was awarded a much-deserved posthumous GC in 1946 'in recognition of most conspicuous gallantry in carrying out hazardous work in a very brave manner'. The fact that he had voluntarily surrendered, for whatever reason, would effectively block award of the VC.

'Friendly Fire'

A/Flt Sgt Arthur Aaron RAF. Tpr Christopher Finney GC

A/Flt Sgt Arthur 'Art' Louis Aaron, a 21-year-old with a passion for rock climbing and flying, was a Stirling bomber pilot with 218 'Gold Coast' Squadron at Downham Market, Norfolk. His quiet determination in the air had already gained him the DFM for pressing on to bomb the target with a flak-crippled aircraft, before nursing it home. Another time Aaron limped back after his Stirling was set on fire by incendiaries falling from another bomber. He ensured that each member of the crew had some experience of the work of the others. They fought together as a highly professional team.

Art Aaron flew his final mission in August 1943. He and his crew had completed twenty sorties over Europe. Sir Arthur Harris, C-in-C Bomber Command, afterwards told his parents: 'In my opinion, never even in the annals of the RAF has the VC been awarded for skill, determination and courage in the face of the enemy of a higher order than that displayed by your son on his last flight.' They took off for the long haul over the Alps to Turin on the 12th. Aaron began their bomb run at 01.20 on Friday 13th. Suddenly tracer ripped through the windscreen and fuselage as a Stirling passed beneath, its rear gunner raking the bomber with his four MGs. The navigator died instantly. Flight engineer Sgt Malcolm Mitchem turned to Aaron. 'It was a dreadful sight. He had been hit in the side of the face. His oxygen mask had gone and I thought that the whole of his jaw had been shot off. His right arm was almost severed at the elbow and he had been wounded in the chest. Yet somehow . . . he had the forethought to signal me to take over.'

Aaron was carried amidships, conscious but unable to speak. Scrawling on the back of the flight log, he told bomb aimer Allan Larden to head for England, refusing morphine until he indicated OK. With the throttle pedestal wrecked, it was impossible to alter the 'cruise' settings of the inboard engines, and the starboard outer was hit and losing power. The elevator control was damaged, the pilot's side of the front screen had disintegrated and the instrument panel was scrap. The automatic pilot was shot up, and ruptured hydraulics left front and rear turrets inoperable. Downham Market was 600 miles away across the Alps and unthinkable. The R/T set worked intermittently. Their distress call was answered by Bone airfield in North Africa, instructing them to over-fly Sicily and land there. They dumped their bombs. Aaron regained consciousness to scribble 'how navigate', before relapsing. There followed nearly four hours of flight over the Mediterranean before sighting Bone. Aaron returned to consciousness as the morphia's effect faded. Amazingly, he rolled on to his knees and insisted on being carried back to the cockpit. Mesmerised, the crew eased him into his seat beside Larden. Aaron piloted the aircraft, communicating by nods and shakes of the head as Larden fired questions and handled the throttles. The radio came alive, warning of a crashed Wellington at the end of the runway. Aaron made four attempts to land before Mitchem shouted on the fifth that they had to get down, there was no more fuel. Through a fog of agony and perhaps losing his reason, Aaron began to pull on the throttles. In desperation Larden had to force him to let go before making a dramatic wheels-up landing. Unknown to them all, a 4,000lb bomb had failed to release and was on its rack beneath them as they crash-landed.

Aaron was rushed to the base hospital where two bullets were removed from his chest. The crew prayed silently. There was a brief rally, but he died in mid-afternoon. The raw courage of Art Aaron in his terrible suffering and devotion to duty is humbling. The citation for his posthumous VC cited an enemy night-fighter as responsible. The air historian Chaz Bowyer, who established its true cause, was vilified by the head of the Air Historical Branch for contradicting Aaron's citation. Thieves stole his medals in August 1946, shocking his widow into a severe illness. They were returned after a nationwide appeal.

* * *

To categorise incoming fire on the battlefield as 'friendly' or 'hostile' as a basis for deciding gallantry awards seems irrational. Lethal fire is – lethal. The reactions of those involved should logically be the sole consideration. As already noted, award of the VC is explicitly confined to acts 'in the presence of the enemy'. In Flt Sgt Aaron's case enemy fire was blamed, doubtless to avoid giving Germany a propaganda windfall. However, Aaron was unquestionably in the presence of the enemy, even if not confronted by him.

It is pertinent to contrast the basis of his much-deserved award with a 'friendly fire' incident sixty years later in the Iraq desert which earned Tpr Christopher Finney the honour of the George Cross. On 28 March 2003 during the invasion by Coalition Forces, 'D' Squadron of the Household Cavalry was probing forward north of Basra, 30km ahead of the main force. In the words of Finney's citation: 'They had been at the forefront of action against enemy armour for several hours.' The squadron's leading vehicles were then mistakenly shot up by two American A10 'tank busters'. Trooper Finney re-entered his blazing Scimitar regardless of its exploding ammunition and pulled his gunner to safety. His senior officers being injured, he returned to the burning and highly dangerous vehicle to radio a situation report. The fighters struck again, wounding 18-year-old Finney in the back and legs and hitting another Scimitar. He then attempted to rescue its driver, but the flames, exploding rounds and his own injuries proved too much. He was awarded the George Cross for his clear-headed courage and devotion.

Like Flt Sgt Aaron, Tpr Finney was on active operations in the presence of the enemy. And like Aaron, he was responding to 'friendly fire'. Only the outcomes differed. A VC for Finney would have deeply offended Washington. It would also have encouraged unwelcome debate on past instances of VC and GC awards that hinged on definition of 'the presence', with varying interpretations over the years.

Burma, Kohima-Imphal, March–July 1944

L/Cpl John Harman. Rifleman Ganju Lama

The 'forgotten' war in the Far East was fought in unspeakable conditions against a fanatical, courageous and cruel enemy. The close-quarter fighting around Kohima and Imphal in North East India in 1944 marked the beginning of the end for Japan's Burma campaign.

L/Cpl John Pennington Harman of the Queen's Own Royal West Kents commanded a section of a forward platoon at Kohima on 8 April. Overnight the enemy had established a machine-gun post only 50yd away, which menaced his company, and intervening ground obstructed the fire of his section on to it. Without hesitation Harman went forward alone, releasing the lever of a four-second grenade and holding it for at least two before hurling it into the post and charging straight after it. He annihilated the enemy and returned with the machine gun. The following morning he recovered a position on a forward slope 150yd from the enemy in order to strengthen a platoon that had been heavily attacked during the night. Returning to his position, he discovered a party of enemy digging in under cover of MG fire and snipers. He ordered his Bren-gun crew to give him covering fire and charged the post alone with fixed bayonet, shooting four and bayoneting another, wiping out the post. Walking back, Harman took a burst of machine-gun fire in his side and died shortly after reaching his lines.

John Harman came from a wealthy family that owned Lundy Isle. A commission was his for the asking, but he had refused it. As his mates fought to stem the bleeding his last words were 'I got the lot – it was worth it'. He was rightly honoured with a posthumous VC.

By June the 14th Army was making progress around Kohima-Imphal, but the enemy was not yet on the run. The Japanese fiercely attacked positions near Ningthoukhong, driving in the perimeter and saturating the ground with tank and medium MG fire. B Company 1/7 Gurkha Rifles was ordered to counter-attack but was pinned down almost immediately. Rifleman Ganju Lama MM, aged 21 from Sikkim, crawled forward on his own initiative with a shoulder-fired PIAT in withering cross-fire and engaged the three tanks single-handed. Despite a broken left wrist and wounds to his right hand and a leg, he got to within 30yd of them and knocked out two, the third being destroyed by an anti-tank gun. He then moved forward and killed or wounded the crews, enabling his company to push on. His achievement in firing the PIAT despite his severe hand injuries is astonishing. Fortunately the heavily sprung weapon re-cocks automatically after the first shot. Ganju Lama received the Cross and reached the rank of Subedar Major, the senior Gurkha Officer in a battalion. He was appointed Honorary ADC to the President of Sikkim for life.

Bomber Command, April 1944

Flt Sgt Norman Jackson RAFVR

A most exceptional VC was gained by Flt Sgt Norman Jackson of 106 Squadron for his action over Schweinfurt on the night of 26 April 1944. The 25-year-old from Ealing was flight engineer of a Lancaster that had just turned for home after bombing a ball-bearing factory when it was heavily strafed by a Fw190. The attack left the starboard wing on fire close to a fuel tank between the fuselage and the inner engine. Despite shrapnel wounds to his shoulder and right leg, Jackson volunteered to climb out and extinguish it before it brought them down. Stuffing a hand fire extinguisher inside his Mae West, he opened his parachute to provide a safety line that the bomb-aimer and navigator could hang on to in case he slipped. He then scrambled out of a hatch and onto the wing in an Arctic-cold 200mph slipstream, the flames fanning back towards him. Jackson gripped the air intake on the leading edge with one hand and fought the fire with the other as flame seared his hands, face and clothes. The fighter returned, putting in a burst that left two bullets in his legs and swept him off the plane. His crewmates frantically paid out the parachute, which caught fire as it swept across the wing. The pilot, Flg Off Fred Mifflin, ordered the crew to abandon the aircraft.

Jackson was at 20,000ft with a smouldering canopy, some holes enlarging as he watched. Miraculously it got him down to a hard landing and a broken ankle. His condition was pitiable, crippled and with severe burns, useless hands and shrapnel injuries. Fred Mifflin and the rear gunner were killed. Jackson and the rest of the crew were captured. After a long recuperation he was sent to a POW compound adjoining Bergen–Belsen concentration camp. He and Gp Capt Leonard Cheshire found themselves the only VCs at their investiture at the Palace. With characteristic generosity, Cheshire tried to get the King to honour Jackson first, as having stuck his neck out the furthest. Even if he had put the fire out, he knew he could never re-enter the aircraft. His sense of duty and willing self-sacrifice was second to none. Norman Jackson had completed his tour of thirty missions, but agreed to stay with the crew, for whom this was their thirtieth. He died in 1994. Ten years later, after the death of Alma his widow, his Cross was sold for a record £235,250 against a pre-auction estimate of £130,000.

D-Day, 6 June 1944

CSM Stanley Hollis

The first VC of the land invasion of Europe was gained by Company Sgt-Maj Stanley Elton Hollis of 6th Battalion, The Green Howards. As a dispatch rider at Dunkirk in 1940 he had taken a wrong turn through an area of Lille just vacated by the Germans. Passing a cul-de-sac, he saw there the still-warm bodies of over 100 French men, women and children. They had been machine-gunned. From that moment his war had become personal and pressing.

The immediate objective of the 6th on D-Day, 6 June 1944, was capture of the Mont Fleury battery's four 150mm guns in concrete casements overlooking Gold Beach. Stanley Hollis was CSM of D Company under Maj Ronald Lofthouse. They were among the first to land. Their route lay 500yd up a beach exit lane, at the end of which Lofthouse and Hollis spotted a sunken pillbox bypassed by the company. The fire-slit topped with bracken was barely above ground and its Spandaus were trained on the rear platoons advancing on the battery. The two were 20yd from it when its MGs opened fire. Hollis rushed forward firing his Sten gun and before the surprised occupants could respond he was on the roof above them. Replacing the magazine and arming a grenade, he crossed to locate the doorway below before bombing it and rushing inside, Sten blazing. Two defenders were killed, three seriously wounded and five more surrendered. Hollis handed them over before reloading and following a communication trench to a two-storey bunker 100yd away. There he took the surrender of its garrison of 18–20 Germans without a fight. He had saved his company from being hit badly from the rear, enabling it to neutralise the battery and open the main beach exit.

Later that day near the village of Crépon the company was securing the road south. Checking a farmyard, Hollis came under sniper fire from a position 100yd off in a hedge that screened a field gun and crew with Spandaus. Lofthouse ordered him to provide fire cover for an assault on the position. Hollis collected a PIAT and two Bren-gunners, and when the movement was held up he pushed forward to engage the gun from a house at 50yd range. The sniper's next bullet grazed his cheek, before the gun traversed and fired a round into the house, partly demolishing it. Hollis moved his party to an alternative position, by which time two members of the enemy gun crew had been killed. The gun was destroyed shortly afterwards. Hollis withdrew, ordering his men to follow. While he was reporting to Lofthouse, the rattle of a Bren indicated the two men had not pulled back. Hollis collected a Bren gun and returned to the position in full view and under fire. During a lull he charged, firing from the hip and shouting to the gunners to withdraw. When they were clear, he followed under heavy fire, arriving back unscratched. On 19 July, however, he was badly wounded in the left leg and ankle and was returned home. Stanley Hollis was decorated by the King, later remarking: 'What I did was nothing to do with courage. I just got mad at seeing all my mates go down around me.'

Italy, October 1944

Pte Ernest Alvia Smith

Hard fighting in Italy throughout the second half of 1944 saw the Allies penetrate Germany's formidable Gothic Line north of Pisa. Reaching the Savio river in October, a Canadian brigade was ordered to establish a bridgehead. The attack was spearheaded by the Seaforth Highlanders of Canada, who crossed the river on the 21st with light weapons and secured their objectives in torrential rain. The river rose 6ft in 5 hours, its soft vertical banks making bridging impossible and preventing tanks and anti-tank guns from getting across to support the rifle companies. The Germans swiftly counter-attacked the right-hand company with three Panther tanks, two self-propelled guns and about thirty infantry.

When the situation became critical, Pte Ernest 'Smoky' Smith, 30, a peacetime labourer from New Westminster, BC, led his PIAT group of two men across an open field under heavy tank fire. Leaving one man on the weapon, he led the other to the road, where they obtained another PIAT. Soon afterwards a Panther appeared, firing its MGs along the line of ditches and wounding his comrade. Smith rose in full view of the tank only 30ft away and fired the PIAT, its hollow charge disabling the vehicle. As ten German infantry leapt off the back and levelled Schmeissers, he killed four point-blank with a tommy gun before driving the others off. A following tank opened fire and more infantry closed in on Smith's position. He steadfastly held on until the enemy withdrew in disorder. Another tank and two self-propelled guns lay destroyed by the Seaforths when a third Panther appeared, sweeping the area with fire. Showing complete disregard, Smith dragged his wounded chum behind a building and obtained medical aid. He then returned to his roadside position to await further probes. There were none. The battalion was able to consolidate its bridgehead. Ernest Smith was rewarded with the Cross. He died aged 91 in August 2005. Ninety-four Canadians have gained VCs, since when Canada has instituted her own awards. The Cross is unchanged save that the motto is in Latin. It has not yet been awarded.

X-craft, Johore Straits, 31 July 1945

Lt Ian Fraser RNR. A/LS James Magennis RN

Lieutenant Ian 'Tich' Fraser commanded HM Midget Submarine XE-3, a craft so small that even at 5ft 4in he could not stand upright in her. She was one of six X-craft dispatched with specially selected four-man crews to the Far East at the end of 1944. The subs had a 1,000-mile range and a top speed of 6 knots. In July 1945 Fraser was briefed to sink the *Takao*, a Japanese heavy cruiser moored in Johore Strait, Singapore. XE-3 was towed 600 miles by submarine to the Straits, where he dropped the tow for the final 80-mile passage to the anchorage. He decided to enter mined waters rather than risk detection in the 'safe' channel, which was certain to be acoustically monitored. After a hair-raising run past hydrophone positions, over loops and through controlled minefields, Fraser penetrated an anti-submarine boom and entered the shallow anchorage on 31 July. He was rather disconcerted on raising the periscope about 400yd from the cruiser to be confronted by the hull of a crowded Japanese navy liberty boat only 10ft away. He could even see passengers' lip movements. Ian Fraser was ever afterwards amazed to have got away with it; the periscope was not noticed. They were forced to scrape along the seabed with only 10ft of water above them to reach *Takao*. The cruiser was almost aground fore and aft with only 5ft clearance midships. While manoeuvring Fraser recalls an almighty crash as they collided with the cruiser and fouled its anchor cable, followed by 'ten terrible minutes' at full power before they broke free, still undiscovered. It took another thirty minutes before they successfully rammed the sub into the gap beneath the hull.

The next task was to fit limpet mines and lay the main charge directly beneath the ship for maximum effect. LS James Joseph Magennis, the diver, was unable fully to open his hatch against *Takao*'s side. He struggled out, damaging an air seal in his breathing apparatus. The oxygen leakage left a revealing line of bubbles on the surface as he worked. He had to scrape away a thick layer of barnacles before attaching the heavy limpets in pairs by a line passed under the cruiser's keel. Adhesion of the magnets was not helped by the hull's profile. When at last the exhausted Magennis re-entered XE-3, the tide was falling so fast that the sub would not budge. They faced the prospect of the 9,800-ton cruiser settling on top of them, to await their mutual destruction as the mines blew. Frantic efforts to break free finally succeeded. Fraser then attempted to jettison the bulky limpet carriers on the sub's exterior, one of which would not release. Magennis insisted despite his exhaustion and the leaking air line that he should leave the craft to free it rather than a less experienced crewman. He succeeded after seven agonising minutes with every prospect of discovery. Fraser again overcame the chain of hazards on the run back, returning the sub to the open sea and recovery.

The *Takao* was crippled thanks to the relentless determination of Ian Fraser, Joseph Magennis and the others to complete their task to perfection regardless of all circumstances. Ian Fraser was a surviving holder of the VC shortly before publication of this book. Jimmy Magennis was the only man from Northern Ireland to be awarded a VC in the Second World War. The public gave £3,066 in appreciation of his heroism, but to its shame the Unionist-dominated council of Belfast refused the Roman Catholic Magennis the freedom of the city. A small official photograph was tucked away in the robing room of the Council Chamber.

The injustice was righted nearly fifty-five years later, after his death, when a fine memorial was unveiled in the City Hall's grounds. The Lord Mayor declared that the Unionist councillors of 1999 had paid off a debt of religious and political shame laid on their backs by their forefathers. The ceremony was attended by Magennis's brother and family, and by skipper Ian Fraser. In honouring one of Belfast's finest sons, the city marked its commitment to the principles for which Magennis had fought so bravely.

9

Final Salutes

I didn't know I had been singled out. There were other guys doing what I did, mates you knew you could rely on. If you looked behind, they were right behind you. They fought shoulder to shoulder, never let you down.

(Bill Speakman VC, recalling the action in Korea that gained him the Cross. The Times, 8 July 2003)

Of the twelve VCs gained since the Second World War, six were awarded posthumously. Four were earned in Korea and four in Vietnam, one in Sarawak, two in the Falklands War and one after the invasion of Iraq.

THE KOREAN WAR, 1950–1953

Maj Kenneth Muir. Pte William Speakman

About 100,000 British and Commonwealth troops, many of them British National Servicemen, fought with US and other forces in response to a UN appeal to stem China's invasion of North Korea in June 1950. The first Cross was awarded posthumously to Maj Kenneth Muir, 1st Battalion, The Argyle and Sutherland Highlanders. He gallantly rallied a situation from near-disaster on Hill 282 near Songju on 23 September 1950. The hill was taken in a dawn attack by two companies of Argyles. By 11.00 enemy mortar and shell fire and raiding parties had inflicted heavy casualties. The remaining members of the two companies were intermixed and in need of unified command. Maj Muir, who had earlier brought up a stretcher party to recover the wounded, took command. He circled the perimeter encouraging the men to stand fast, ignoring continuous fire and entreaties to take cover. Recognition panels laid out for an air strike did not prevent aircraft hitting the Argyle's position hard. Fire bombs and machine-gun fire forced a withdrawal to a position 50ft below the crest.

Retreat would have been fully justified. Only thirty fighting men remained, with little ammunition. Instead, Muir and the three surviving officers formed a small force that he personally led in a counter-attack. To understand fully the implication of this it is necessary to realise how demoralising the effect of the air strike had been. All ranks rallied magnificently and the crest was secured. Thereafter Muir's actions were beyond praise. Grossly outnumbered, he moved about under heavy automatic fire distributing the last of the ammunition and maintaining fire cover to enable the many wounded to be got away. When his own ammunition ran out, he used a 2in mortar with deadly effect for five precious minutes before he was caught by two bursts from machine guns. Kenneth Muir's last words were: 'The gooks will never drive the Argyles off this Hill.' The effect of his leadership was amazing. All the wounded were evacuated and it was later discovered that very heavy casualties had been inflicted on the enemy.

The action of Pte William 'Bill' Speakman of The Black Watch is legendary. On United Hill on 4 November 1951 the 1st Battalion King's Own Scottish Borderers, to which he was attached, was attacked at dusk by continuous waves of the enemy. Speakman collected a party of six men and satchels of grenades and led them in charge after charge for over two hours, breaking up a succession of assaults and inflicting very heavy casualties. Serious wounds did not stop him. The huge 6ft 7in Private from Altrincham allegedly threw beer bottles when to hand. He recalled to *The Times*:

It was getting dark and we could only just pick them out. They came at us in a rush all along the front. There was a lot of hand-to-hand. . . . They were milling around you – you can't even pull your bolt back, so you fight with the butt of your rifle and bayonet. The battle went on for six hours. When we ran out of ammunition we started to throw rocks and stones and anything else we could lay our hands on. I led up to fifteen counter-charges – we had to get our wounded. We couldn't just give in – we'd fought for so long we just couldn't give up that bloody hill. . . . We were told to withdraw and that's when we went forward to clear the hill, to get our wounded off. . . . To be honest you get hit and you don't realise it – you're a bit busy – and someone says 'Bill, you've been hit in the back!' I was ordered off the hill to get my wounds dressed. The medical orderly tending me was caught in a burst and I said 'stuff it' and went forward again.

The company was ordered to withdraw at 21.00 in the face of continuing enemy machine gun and mortar fire and grenades. Speakman led a final charge to clear the hill's crest. He and his sadly depleted party held it while the remainder of his Company retired. He had so dominated the situation throughout that he inspired his comrades to stand firm and fight the enemy to a standstill. Speakman's was the first VC to be invested by Queen Elizabeth II. After retirement, as a Sergeant, in 1969, he eventually settled in South Africa, selling his medals for £1,500. They were eventually sold on for £20,000. He was a surviving holder of the VC shortly before publication of this book.

THE VIETNAM WAR, 1959–1975

WOII Keith Payne

The US in Vietnam were supported by a small force of Australian troops, including a specialist training team working with the South Vietnamese army. All four VCs of this war were gained by 'The Team', the first going to WOII Kevin Wheatley (see pp. 67–70). The fourth was gained by WOII Keith Payne from Ingham, Queensland. On 24 May 1969 in Kon Tum Province WO Payne was a company commander with 1st Mobile Strike Force Battalion, a Vietnamese unit, when it was attacked by a North Vietnamese force in superior strength. The enemy isolated the two lead companies, one of which was Payne's, and with heavy mortar and rocket support assaulted their position from three directions simultaneously. The indigenous soldiers began to fall back. Directly exposing himself to fire, Payne temporarily held off the assaults by alternately using his weapon and running from position to position collecting grenades and throwing them at the enemy. While doing this he was wounded in the hands and arms. Despite his continuing efforts, the Force gave way under increasing pressure, and the battalion commander, together with several advisers and a few soldiers, withdrew.

Ignoring his wounds and the extremely heavy fire, WO Payne covered their withdrawal by again throwing grenades and firing his weapon as the enemy attempted to follow up. Still under attack, he then ran across exposed ground to head off his own troops, who were withdrawing in disorder. He successfully stopped them and organised the remnants of his and the second company into a temporary defensive perimeter by nightfall. Having achieved this, Payne at great personal risk moved out into the darkness alone in an attempt to find the wounded and other soldiers. Some had been left on the previous position and others were scattered in the area. Although the enemy was still occupying the position, Payne crawled back to it and extricated several wounded men. He then continued to search the area, in which the enemy was also moving and firing, for some three hours.

He collected forty lost soldiers, some wounded, and returned with this group to the temporary perimeter he had left, only to find that the remainder of the battalion had withdrawn.

Undeterred by this setback and personally assisting the seriously wounded American adviser, he led the group through the enemy to the safety of his battalion base. His coolness and superb leadership saved the lives of many indigenous soldiers and several of his fellow advisers.

Payne received his VC from the Queen aboard the Royal Yacht *Britannia* in Brisbane. He was a surviving holder shortly before publication of this book. In all, ninety-six Australians have been awarded the Victoria Cross.

MALAYSIA–INDONESIA CONFRONTATION, 1963–1966

L/Cpl Rambahadur Limbu

The action of L/Cpl Rambahadur Limbu must rank as one of the most outstanding examples of personal courage to have gained the VC. Indonesia triggered a confrontation with the newly formed Federation of Malaysia from 1963 to 1966 by attempting to seize its territory in Sarawak and Borneo. Rambahadur and his company of the 2nd/10th Gurkha Rifles was operating in the Bau district of Sarawak near the Indonesian border in 1965. He won his Cross in a clash with Indonesian forces there on 21 November.

The company discovered the enemy firmly entrenched in platoon strength on top of a sheer hill approachable only along a knife-edge ridge. Spotting a sentry guarding this route with a machine gun, Rambahadur led two riflemen up the ridge, inching to within 10yd of the sentry, who then saw them and opened fire, wounding one of the party. Rambahadur rushed forward through the machine-gun fire, killed the sentry and occupied the trench, gaining a vital first foothold on the objective. Disregarding heavy automatic fire, which was now directed onto the trench from further along the hilltop, he moved his group to a better position some yards ahead. The deafening noise of exploding grenades and machine-gun fire prevented shouted communication with his officer. Rambahadur moved into the open in defiance of both his own comrades' and the incoming fire, and reported personally. As he did so he saw both his riflemen become seriously wounded.

Knowing the two men had to be evacuated immediately, Rambahadur made the first of three almost suicidal attempts to recover them. For three minutes he crawled forward under intense fire from at least two machine-gun posts, which could not be engaged at that stage by the rest of his platoon. When almost able to grasp the first casualty he was driven back by the weight of fire, only to start crawling up yet again. It was painfully clear that he had no chance at that speed. He rushed forward, throwing himself beside the injured man before carrying him to safety with fire support from two machine guns that had reached a position to his right. Rambahadur then turned back and repeated the climb, the enemy concentrating all its efforts on him. In a series of short rushes he reached the position and quite miraculously made it back unscathed with the second man. This gallant action had lasted 20 minutes. For all but a few seconds of that time L/Cpl Rambahadur had been moving alone in full view of the enemy and under the continuous aimed fire of their automatic weapons. His complete contempt for them, and his utter disregard of his own life in saving that of his comrades, inspired all who witnessed it.

Rambahadur recovered the machine gun and used it to kill four more of the enemy. In the hour-long battle at least twenty-four of them were killed at a cost to the Gurkhas of three killed and two wounded. His pleasure on learning of his award was overshadowed by the death of his young wife the day after his return to Singapore. She had been ill after the birth of their second son. At the Queen's personal request he flew to London with his 5-year-old son Bhakta to receive the VC at Buckingham Palace. He was appointed one of Her Majesty's Gurkha Orderly Officers in 1983, and retired in 1985 with the honorary rank of captain.

Rambahadur Limbu was a surviving holder of the VC shortly before publication of this book.

THE FALKLANDS WAR, 1982

Lt-Col Herbert Jones. Sgt Ian McKay. Pte Stephen Illingsworth DCM

Argentina invaded the Falkland Islands on 2 April 1982 in 'Operation Azul' to reclaim territory they believed was theirs. Four days later a considerable Task Force sailed from England to remove them. The ensuing land, sea and air operations were hard fought and costly for both sides before the invaders surrendered on 14/15 June.

The campaign secured posthumous VCs for Lt-Col Herbert Jones – universally known as Colonel 'H' – commanding the 2nd Battalion The Parachute Regiment, and Sgt Ian McKay, 3rd Battalion. 'H' Jones had been ordered to take Goose Green and Darwin in the first land battle of the conflict. 'A' Company of 2 Para was held up at first light on 28 May by a well-positioned enemy in company strength on a ridge. The base of a re-entrant leading to the Argentine position was eventually taken by a forward section that lost several killed in the action. Jones brought forward his small Tactical HQ party under smoke cover and continued on up the rising ground regardless of heavy enemy small arms fire. They reached a point broadly level with the Argentines' weapons pits. Jones was now at the very front of his Battalion.

Lt Thurman RM accompanied the HQ party. His eyewitness report records Jones's increasing frustration with the poor accuracy of the supporting mortar section in this phase, and the developing stalemate. The Battalion was further handicapped by the absence of indirect fire support from the Navy. After more than an hour of fierce but unrewarding exchanges with the enemy, whose artillery fire was intensifying, Jones lost his temper, according to Thurman. Seizing a sub-machine gun, 'H' called on those around him and charged the nearest enemy position 10 or 20yd ahead. He must have known that he would draw fire from six or seven bunkers. One man followed, whether to stop or support Jones is unclear, but he was hit immediately in a burst of automatic fire. Jones also fell, apparently a stumble, regained his feet and moved forward firing short bursts until hit low in the neck and killed. Soon afterwards 2 Para took the position, the enemy quickly surrendering. Darwin and Goose Green were liberated and some 1,200 Argentinians were captured. The battle cost 17 British dead and about 40 wounded. Argentine losses were 45 dead and some 90 wounded.

The recommendations of senior officers for award of the VC can range from a simple 'recommended', through 'strongly' to 'very strongly'. The standard to be applied includes a 90 per cent possibility of being killed in performing the deed. Recommendations pass to the VC Committee for the relevant Service, normally three senior officers and the Permanent Under Secretary at the Ministry of Defence. A separate tri-service committee, chaired by Adm Sir Desmond Cassidi, the Second Sea Lord, had been formed by the Ministry 'to adjudicate on overall standards and to monitor the number of awards by grades to each Service [arising from the Falklands conflict]'.

Anticipating future doubts about the wisdom of Lt-Col Jones's action, Lt-Gen Sir Roland Guy, the Military Secretary and Secretary to the VC Committee, minuted the committee:

It can be argued that Jones's action was reckless and that at a critical moment in the attack he needlessly risked his life and showed a lack of judgement rather than conspicuous bravery. It is clear from the citation, however, that his action, which epitomises the determination, drive and offensive spirit which exemplified his leadership of the Battalion, was committed at what was the critical and pivotal moment of the battle; that its effect upon the enemy and his own Battalion was decisive and that such action was necessary at that moment to break the stalemate which had already lasted an hour or more.

The Second Sea Lord's committee took the same view. Lt-Gen Sir Richard Trant, the Task Force Land Commander, had 'very strongly recommended' a posthumous VC. Adm Sir John Fieldhouse, in overall command, had 'only' given Lt-Col Jones a 'recommended'. The VC Committee considered a posthumous Military Cross at one point, but the overriding view was that Lt-Col Jones initiated 'the key action at a moment of stalemate which probably unlatched the gate to further momentum and ultimate success'.

Two weeks later, on the night of 11/12 June, 3 Para supported by HMS *Avenger* mounted an assault on the Argentinian 7th Infantry Regiment. In the bloodiest battle of the war, lasting most of the night, the Argentines on Mount Longdon were driven off in bitter fighting. Sgt Ian McKay led 4 Platoon, B Company, in a silent attack on an Argentine battalion on the slopes overlooking Port Stanley. When the initial objective was secured, he was ordered to clear part of a long ridge held in considerable strength by a well-positioned and determined enemy. The platoon came under very heavy MG fire from several positions on the ridge, causing casualties. Its commander, Lt Bickerdike, ordered it to seek shelter among rocks on the ridge itself. There it met part of 5 Platoon.

Enemy fire remained heavy and accurate. Their position became 'hazardous', according to McKay's citation. Taking McKay, Cpl Bailey and a few others, and supported by covering fire, Bickerdike moved forward to reconnoitre. When he was almost immediately hit in the leg, command passed to Sgt McKay, who decided on immediate action if the advance was not to falter. He changed the recce to an assault, quietly ordering covering fire while the rest were to skirmish forward.

Enemy tracer was richocheting all around them as they advanced through the rocks. As they headed for muzzle flashes, Pte Burt was killed in the hail of fire and Cpl Bailey and Pte Logan fell wounded. McKay went on alone, reaching the position and dispatching the enemy with grenades. He was shot and killed at the moment of victory, his body falling across the bunker he had just cleared.

Sgt Ian McKay's perseverance and gallant leadership relieved the beleaguered 4 and 5 Platoons, who redeployed relatively safely. He had retrieved a most dangerous situation and was instrumental in ensuring the success of the attack. Lt-Gen Sir Richard Trant accorded him a 'very strong' recommendation for the Cross; Adm Fieldhouse a 'recommended'.

A third member of the Regiment was recommended for the VC for his courage and inspiration to others in first rescuing a wounded comrade while exposed under intense fire, and soon afterwards dying at the hands of a sniper when attempting to retrieve his webbing equipment containing much-needed ammunition. Pte Stephen Illingsworth fell at Goose Green only a few hours after Col 'H' Jones. In the event he was posthumously awarded the Distinguished Conduct Medal. Although he had been strongly recommended for the Cross by Lt-Gen Sir Richard Trant and Adm Sir John Fieldhouse, they nevertheless emphasised that Lt-Col Jones and Sgt McKay had Priority 1 against Priority 3 for Pte Illingsworth.

A note of caution was raised by Lt-Gen Sir Roland Guy, who advised the Committee that, while Illingsworth's actions were heroic and selfless and epitomised the very best of soldierly qualities, 'his action does not match the standard of action of Jones and McKay'. The Second Sea Lord may have taken a similar line, though his remarks on standards have been blanked out on the WO file. His views on eligibility for the supreme award were robust, having just referred back a VC recommendation for a Lt-Cdr which he considered not strong enough. As chairman of the tri-service Committee his comments may have prompted Lt-Gen Guy's further advice to the VC Committee to contrast the three Falklands recommendations before them for the Paras, with the two VCs awarded the 1st Bn, Gloucester Regiment after the Imjin River battle in Korea in 1952. Guy continued:

> It is not for the VC Committee to make any judgement on what would be the appropriate number of VCs to award for this campaign in comparison with the numbers that have been awarded in past campaigns. . . . However, there will inevitably be great public interest over whether the award is in any way being cheapened if an excessive number are awarded. (TNA: PRO WO373/188)

IRAQ, 2004

Pte Johnson Beharry

The American-led Coalition Force invaded Iraq in March 2003. The British Army was tasked to secure the southern sector centred on Basra. A swift and resolute drive on Baghdad overcame organised resistance in five weeks to end Saddam Hussein's vile reign. The Coalition was totally unprepared, however, for the ensuing murderous insurgency, crippling a proud but dangerously fragmented nation most of whom want only peace and the chance to build on their new freedoms. Coalition troops remain to support the creation of an elected government and an adequate home defence force.

Pte Johnson Gideon Beharry, 25, of the 1st Battalion The Princess of Wales's Royal Regiment, gained his VC, the most recent to be awarded, for repeated gallantry when twice ambushed in the deadly daily business of maintaining some kind of order. On the second occasion a rocket-propelled grenade left him in a coma with life-threatening head injuries. His was the Regiment's 57th Cross. Although formed in 1992, its forebear regiments go back to 1572. The fourth of eight children, Beharry had left Grenada for Britain in 1999.

Twelve Warrior armoured combat vehicles of Beharry's company undertook a night operation on 1 May 2004 to replenish a Coalition Force outpost in the troubled city of Al Amarah. As they neared it, six vehicles were redirected to extract a foot patrol pinned down under fire. When those ran into a series of ambushes, Beharry's platoon with the remaining Warriors was diverted to assist. His commander, 2/Lt Richard Deane, took the lead with Beharry driving and gunners manning the 30mm cannon and a 7.62mm chain gun. There were several soldiers in the back. When the road became strangely deserted – a sure indicator of trouble ahead – Deane ordered a halt to assess the situation. Seconds later his Warrior was blasted by multiple rocket-propelled grenade strikes. Those behind later reported seeing the 30-ton vehicle engulfed and visibly rocked by violent explosions.

Beharry saw yet another RP grenade heading straight for him. It struck as he tried to close his hatch, overpressure from the charge tearing the cover from his grip. The blast passed directly above him, further injuring the semi-conscious gunner. His armoured periscope destroyed, Beharry had to cover the last 1,500m with the hatch opened up and his head exposed to the enemy. As the burning vehicle raced through a tunnel of fire, it was again struck by grenades and small arms rounds, one bullet actually penetrating Beharry's helmet and lodging inside.

Spotting another Warrior from C Company, Beharry followed it to the besieged outpost. There he hauled first Lt Deane and then the gunner from the turret and into the relative safety of another vehicle, completely disregarding incoming small-arms fire. He returned to the rear of his own vehicle to lead the disoriented and shocked men and casualties to safety before re-entering the still-burning Warrior and driving it inside the perimeter of the outpost, thus denying it to the enemy. Only then did Beharry pull the fire extinguisher handles, immobilising his diesel engine. Once inside another Warrior he collapsed from the sheer physical and mental exhaustion of his efforts.

Returning to duty on 11 June, Beharry was part of a quick reaction force ordered to cut off an insurgents' mortar team in Al Amarah. As lead vehicle his Warrior was moving fast through dark streets towards the suspected firing point when it was ambushed from rooftop positions. An RPG-7 detonated on the vehicle's frontal armour just 6in from Beharry's head, very severely injuring it. More rockets struck the turret and sides of the vehicle, incapacitating his commander and wounding several others. Concussed and near-blinded with blood, he nevertheless had the instinctive presence of mind to engage reverse and back out of the area on full throttle until the Warrior slammed into a wall. He then lost consciousness. In getting the vehicle clear he had enabled other crews to extract his personnel with greatly reduced risk.

* * *

During a long convalescence Pte Beharry was gladdened to hear that, when fit, he may go to Afghanistan to train soldiers there. 'That is ideally what I would like to do. The Army is what I know and love, it's the only career for me.' Those few words of pride in his Service, in his own professionalism, and in getting on with the job, speak for the 1,351 men of all arms of the British and Commonwealth forces, and civilians too, who have been awarded the Victoria Cross for their supreme valour, example and achievement.

It remains our simple duty to honour them and preserve their memory.

Bibliography

Place of publication is London unless otherwise specified.

Primary Sources

The National Archives at the Public Record Office

TNA: PRO WO 32 series. War Office administration including many VC files

TNA: PRO WO 32/21740. VC provision and general correspondence (1940–78)

TNA: PRO WO32/16088. Provision of metal for VCs (1942–56)

TNA: PRO WO 373/188. Recommendations for Honours and Awards, Army (1965–80)

TNA: PRO WO 98/3, 4, 8. VC Registers (1856–1944)

TNA: PRO AIR 1, 2, 20 series. Air Forces

TNA: PRO ADM 1, 23, 116 series. Admiralty

TNA: PRO MINT 20/806. VC (1923–56)

TNA: PRO T 160 series. Treasury papers

TNA: PRO T 160/136. Manufacture of the VC by the Royal Mint (January–April 1923)

Secondary Sources

Books

Adkin, Mark, *The Last Eleven*, Leo Cooper, 1991

Arthur, Max, *Symbol of Courage: A History of the Victoria Cross*, Sidgwick & Jackson, 2004

Biggs, Maurice, *The Story of Gurkha VCs*, Winchester, The Gurkha Museum, 2001

Billière, Gen Sir Peter de la, *Supreme Courage: Heroic Stories from 150 Years of the Victoria Cross*, Little, Brown, 2004

Bowyer, Chaz, *For Valour: The Air VCs*, Caxton, 2002

Buzzell, Nora, *The Register of the Victoria Cross*, Cheltenham, This England Books, 1981

Clayton, Ann, *Chavasse: Double VC*, Leo Cooper, 1992

Cooksley, Peter G., *The Air VCs*, Stroud, Sutton Publishing, 1996

Creagh, Gen Sir O'Moore, VC, and Humphris, Miss E.M., *The VC and DSO*, vol. I *The Victoria Cross*, Standard Art Book Co., 1920

Crook, M.J., *The Evolution of the Victoria Cross*, Tunbridge Wells, Midas Books, 1975

Fitzherbert, Cuthbert, *Henry Clifford VC*, Michael Joseph, 1956

Laffin, John, *British VCs of World War 2*, Stroud, Sutton Publishing, 1997

Lucas Phillips, C.E., *Victoria Cross Battles of the Second World War*, Heinemann, 1973

Mulholland, John, and Jordan, Alan, *Victoria Cross Bibliography*, Spink & Son, 1999

Parry, D.H., *The VC: Its Heroes and their Valour*, Cassell, rev. edn, 1913

Percival, John, *For Valour, the Victoria Cross*, Thames Methuen, 1986

Perrett, Bryan, *For Valour*, Weidenfeld & Nicolson, 2003

Roe, F. Gordon, *The Bronze Cross*, P.R. Gawthorn, 1945

Shannon, Stephen, *Beyond Praise: The Durham Light Infantrymen who were Awarded the Victoria Cross*, Durham, County Durham Books, 1998

Smyth, Brig The Rt Hon Sir John, VC MP, *The Story of the Victoria Cross 1856–1963*, F. Muller, 1963

Toomey, T.E., *Heroes of the Victoria Cross*, Geo. Newnes, 1895

Turner, John Frayn, *VCs of the Air*, Harrap, 1960

Wilkins, Philip A., *The History of the Victoria Cross*, Constable, 1904

Newspapers and Specialist Publications

The Journal of the Victoria Cross Society, edns 1–6, ed. Brian Best

Sabretache, journal of the Military Historical Society of Australia

The Times, Digital Archive 1785–1985. Also full-text database 1985–

Articles and Papers

Anon., 'The Victoria Cross Cascabel', *Royal Logistics Corps Journal* (October 1997), 358

Anon., 'The VC Centenary Exhibition, Marlborough House', official catalogue (January 1956)

Ashton, Dr J., 'The Analysis of Victoria Crosses in New Zealand', abstract, *ANZAC Fellowship* (1995)

Ashton, Dr J., and Creagh, Prof. D., 'The X-Ray Analysis of Victoria Crosses', *Proceedings, Microscopy, Materials & Techniques Conference, Institute of Metals & Materials, Australasia* (1993), 57–61

Creagh, Prof. D. 'Analytical Studies of the Victoria Crosses in the Custody of the Australian War Memorial', *Sabretache*, 32 (January–March 1991), 15–16

Gilmour, Dr B., 'The Metal of the Victoria Cross: Legend and Reality', abstract, Founders, Smiths & Platers Conference, Oxford, 20–24 September 1999

Smith, R., 'X-Ray Fluorescence of Victoria Crosses', *News from the Broad Arrow Tower*, Royal Armouries, London (November 1985)

Staunton, A., 'Blaming Buckingham Palace: The Thirteen-Month Delay in the Award of the Wheatley Victoria Cross', *Sabretache*, 38 (July–September 1997), 14–20

Timbers, Brig K., 'Victoria Cross: The Origins of the Metal Used in their Manufacture', paper, Royal Artillery Historical Trust (May 1998)

Principal Websites

www.diggerhistory.info
www.gazette-online.co.uk
www.gc-database.co.uk
www.regiments.org
www.victoriacross.net
www.victoriacross.org.uk/vcross.htm
www.victoriacrosssociety.com

Background Reading

Banks, Arthur, *Military Atlas of the First World War*, Heinemann, 1975

Chandler, David, and Beckett, Ian (eds), *The Oxford History of the British Army*, Oxford, Oxford University Press, 1996

Conacher, J.B., *Britain and the Crimea, 1855–56*, Macmillan Press, 1987

Edwardes, Michael, *Red Year: The Indian Rebellion of 1857*, Sphere Books, 1975

Farwell, Byron, *For Queen and Country*, Allen Lane, 1981

Farwell, Byron, *Queen Victoria's Little Wars*, Allen Lane, 1973

Featherstone, Donald, *Weapons and Equipment of the Victorian Soldier*, Arms and Armour Press, 1978

Gilbert, Martin, *The Second World War*, Weidenfeld & Nicolson, 1989

Hibbert, Christopher, *The Destruction of Lord Raglan*, Longmans, Green, 1961

Hill, J.R., *The Oxford Illustrated History of the Royal Navy*, Oxford, Oxford University Press, 1995

James, Lawrence, *The Rise and Fall of the British Empire*, Little, Brown, 1998

Kerr, Paul, *The Crimean War*, Boxtree, 1997

Kinglake, A.W., *The Invasion of the Crimea*, vol. III (1866), vol. IV (1868), vol. V (1875), vol. VI (1880), vol. VII (1882), Edinburgh and London, Blackwood

Lambert, Andrew, and Badsey, Stephen, *The War Correspondents: The Crimean War*, Stroud, Sutton Publishing, 1994

Liddell Hart, Capt B.H., *The Tanks*, 2 vols, Cassell, 1959

Liddell Hart, Capt B.H., *History of the First World War*, Cassell, 1970

Maude, Col F.C., VC, and Sherer, J.W., *Memories of the Mutiny*, 2 vols, 1894

Maurice, Maj R.F.G. (ed), *The Tank Corps Book of Honour*, Spottiswoode, 1919

Mercer, Patrick, *Give Them a Volley and Charge! The Battle of Inkermann, 1854*, Staplehurst, Spellmount, 1998

Packenham, Thomas, *The Boer War*, Weidenfeld & Nicolson, 1979

Sibbald, Raymond, *The War Correspondents: The Boer War*, Stroud, Sutton Publishing, 1993

Smyth, Brig The Rt Hon Sir John, VC MP, *The Story of the George Cross*, Arthur Barker, 1968

Sweetman, John, *The Crimean War*, Botley, Osprey Publishing, 2001

Warner, Philip (ed), *Letters Home from the Crimea*, Witney, Windrush Press, 1999

* * *

Interested readers may care to contact the Victoria Cross Society, which produces a high-quality and authoritative illustrated journal, published twice yearly. Members can purchase back copies, subject to availability.

E-mail: secretary@victoriacrosssociety.com
Website: www.victoriacrosssociety.com

The Secretary
The Victoria Cross Society
Kintons
Harlequin Place
Crowborough
East Sussex
TN6 1HZ
United Kingdom

Index